STARTING WITH MILL

Continuum's *Starting with . . .* series offers clear, concise and accessible introductions to the key thinkers in philosophy. The books explore and illuminate the roots of each philosopher's work and ideas, leading readers to a thorough understanding of the key influences and philosophical foundations from which his or her thought developed. Ideal for first-year students starting out in philosophy, the series will serve as the ideal companion to study of this fascinating subject.

Available now:

Starting with Berkeley, Nick Jones

Starting with Derrida, Sean Gaston

Starting with Descartes, C. G. Prado

Starting with Hegel, Craig B. Matarrese

Starting with Heidegger, Tom Greaves

Starting with Hobbes, George MacDonald Ross

Starting with Nietzsche, Ullrich Haase

Starting with Rousseau, James Delaney

Starting with Sartre, Gail Linsenbard

Forthcoming:

Starting with Hume, Charlotte R. Brown and William Edward Morris

Starting with Kant, Andrew Ward

Starting with Kierkegaard, Patrick Sheil

Starting with Leibniz, Lloyd Strickland

Starting with Locke, Greg Forster

Starting with Merleau-Ponty, Katherine Morris

Starting with Schopenhauer, Sandra Shapshay

Starting with Wittgenstein, Chon Tejedor

STARTING WITH MILL

JOHN R. FITZPATRICK

continuum

Continuum International Publishing Group
The Tower Building
11 York Road
London SE1 7NX

80 Maiden Lane
Suite 704
New York, NY 10038

www.continuumbooks.com

British Library Cataloguing-in-Publication Data
A catalogue record for this book is available from the British Library.

ISBN: HB: 978–1–8470–6239–0
PB: 978–1–8470–6240–6

Library of Congress Cataloguing-in-Publication Data
Fitzpatrick, John R.
Starting with Mill / John R. Fitzpatrick.
p. cm.
Includes bibliographical references (p.) and index.
ISBN 978–1–84706–239–0—ISBN 978–1–84706–240–6 1. Mill, John Stuart, 1806–1873. I. Title.
B1607.F57 2010
192—dc22
2010002044

Typeset by RefineCatch Limited, Bungay, Suffolk
Printed and bound in Great Britain by
the MPG Books Group

CONTENTS

CHRONOLOGY

1806 Born May 20 in Pemberton section of London. First born child of James and Harriet Mill. Named after father's patron Sir John Stuart.
1809 Begins education at home by father with study of Greek.
1814 Begins study of Latin.
1818 James Mill publishes *History of British India*, and is subsequently employed at East India Company.
1820 Goes to France staying with family of Sir Samuel Bentham.
1821 Studies Jeremy Bentham. Begins publishing articles in newspapers. Studies law with John Austin. Studies psychology with his father.
1823 Internship at East India Company. Employment there will last 35 years. Arrested and detained for distribution of birth control pamphlets.
1826 Mental crisis.
1830 Meets Harriet Taylor.
1832 Death of Jeremy Bentham.
1836 Founds and edits *London and Westminster Review*. Death of James Mill. Promoted to assistant examiner.
1838 'Essay on Bentham.'
1843 *A System of Logic*.
1844 *Essays on Some Unsettled Questions in Political Economy*
1846 Writes articles criticizing governmental response to Irish famine.
1848 *Principles of Political Economy*.
1849 Death of John Taylor.
1851 Marries Harriet Taylor.
1856 Promoted to chief examiner.

1857 Indian Mutiny.

1858 Retires from East India Company with generous pension after Parliament assumes direct rule of India. Harriet Taylor Mill dies and is buried in Avignon, France. For the rest of Mill's life he will spend much of each year in Avignon, often accompanied by his step-daughter, Helen Taylor.

1859 *On Liberty*, with dedication to Harriet.

1861 *Considerations on Representative Government. Utilitarianism* (in three installments in *Frazer's Magazine*, as a book two years later).

1865 Elected to Parliament. Elected Lord Rector of St. Andrews University. 'August Compte and Positivism,' *An Examination of the Philosophy of Sir William Hamilton*.

1866 Calls for prosecution of Governor of Jamaica for his unjustified use of military force against Black Jamaican protestors.

1867 Brings forward to Parliament first proposal for women voting.

1868 Loses reelection.

1869 *Subjection of Women*. Edits with assistance from Alexander Bain, George Grote, and Andrew Findlater a second edition of James Mill's *An Analysis of the Phenomena of the Human Mind*.

1873 Dies May 20 in Avignon, France. *Autobiography of John Stuart Mill*, and *Chapters on Socialism* published posthumously by Helen Taylor. She will go on to publish his *Three Essays on Religion*, volume IV of *Dissertations and Discussions*.

PREFACE

There are two main goals I wish to accomplish in this work. The first is to ground Mill solidly in the history of philosophy. To really understand Mill or any other philosopher, one must understand the critical issues of the day, and how that philosopher's views fit into this overall discussion. I have spent the last few years teaching the history of philosophy, and my own sense of what Mill is doing has profited enormously from it. Mill is a product of his times. He is in my view the last figure of an era philosophers call the modern era. But he is also classically educated. So to make sense of Mill, some knowledge of both modern philosophy and ancient philosophy is in order. Of course in one small book I cannot do justice to Socrates, Plato, Aristotle, Descartes, Locke, Hume, Smith, Kant, Bentham, and James Mill. But all of the above play a significant role in this book. Mill's education began with the Ancient Greeks, and his love of Greece never left him. This Grecian influence can be felt throughout the book. Similarly, Mill is an empiricist and a naturalist. Any clear understanding of his ethics and politics has to include at a minimum why he is rejecting rationalism and Kantian transcendental idealism. He has reasons for rejecting a priori morals or moral intuitions. This can be traced back through His Father and Bentham to Locke.

Since my graduate school days I have been interested in the 'two Mills problem.' For at least the last fifty years many philosophers have argued that there are two John Stuart Mills.[1] There is the rights supporting liberal Mill of *On Liberty*, and then there is the author of *Utilitarianism*. This reading often presupposes that there is no possibility of reconciling these two Mills, since it is purportedly impossible to be both a supporter of liberal justice and utilitarianism. On this view, 'liberal utilitarianism' is a full-blooded oxymoron. Eventually I will propose specific readings of *On Liberty* and *Utilitarianism* that make this claim far from credible. I will offer a reading of Mill that suggests that he believes that we do have fundamental rights, and yet still manages to keep this work and Mill's overall moral theory under a utilitarian rubric. However, this will not satisfy sophisticated opponents of utilitarianism. Sophisticated opponents of Utilitarianism will admit that utilitarianism can support some sort of rights, but the system of rights that utilitarianism can support is not sufficient to protect the individual liberties necessary for a liberal theory of justice. They have argued that in utilitarian hands individual rights become so truncated or conditional that the rights defended by utilitarianism do not give individuals the individual protection that an acceptable theory of justice would provide. My second main goal is to argue that this view is mistaken, and properly understood Mill's liberal utilitarianism can support a system of rights rich enough to guarantee individual liberty.

A point of clarification: Some commentators use the term 'liberal' to suggest a supporter of a priori, natural, indefeasible, and/or God-given rights. I am using the term 'liberal' to indicate a supporter of what Gerald Gauss has called the Fundamental Liberty Principle, namely, 'freedom is normatively basic, and so the onus of justification is on those who would limit freedom. It follows from this that political authority and law must be justified, as they limit the liberty of citizens. Consequently, a central question of liberal political theory is whether political authority can be justified, and if so, how.'[2] This does not preclude a belief in, say, a priori rights, but it certainly does not require one. Similarly, I use the term 'rights' broadly and inclusively, since as Gauss notes liberals disagree 'about the concept of liberty, and as a result the liberal ideal of protecting individual liberty can lead to very different conceptions of the task of government'[3] One attempt to define rights broadly and inclusively is offered by Norman E. Bowie and Robert L. Simon in their *The Individual and the Political Order*. These authors suggest that rights should be understood as entitlements or areas of 'individual inviolability that may not be invaded on grounds of benevolence, social utility, the public interest, or charity'[4] As we shall see, Mill's utilitarianism does not prevent him from demarcating an area of personal morality that would allow such entitlements. For Mill's definition of rights see p. 77.

This work is primarily an exegesis of Mill's thought and a defense of his moral and political philosophy from his critics. But moral and political philosophy matters. One might say that moral and political philosophy is the theory and social institutions and government is the practice. There is an old curse, some say Chinese, some say Scottish that goes: 'May you live in interesting times.' And we live in interesting times. Many of the recent failures of government have been consequentialist failures. Who could have imagined terrorists attacking New York, or the insurrection in Iraq, or the ballooning deficit, or the actual cost of drugs for seniors, or the flooding in New Orleans, or . . .? In the aftermath of all these breakdown of social institutions and governmental failures, the relevance of consequentialist thought should be apparent, and the virtues of a liberal utilitarianism obvious. Thus, a defense of Mill's philosophy would be an important project. I hope the reader finds this work a useful first step.

Finally, my sources for the chronology include Mill 1986, Mill 1994, Mill 2008, Skorupski 2006, Capaldi 2004, and Packe 1954 with an assist from my student Anthony Mundis. I would also like to thank my friend from graduate school, Bertis Vanderschaaff, for reading and commenting on parts of this manuscript. My dissertation director, Betsy Postow, died during my work on this manuscript. This work is dedicated to her.

CHAPTER 1

MILL AND THE MODERN WORLD

i. MODERN PHILOSOPHY

Often the best way to begin understanding the work of any philosopher is to understand the historical era of his or her life. Philosophy does not take place in a vacuum. Philosophers are influenced by other thinkers, and the events of their times. It is often the case that without a clear idea of what a philosopher is rejecting, it is exceedingly difficult to see what point is being made. In the case of Mill, this is clearly important. Mill is writing in the nineteenth century, and the nineteenth century is either the culmination of, or a response to, a particularly fruitful era in Western philosophy called 'modern philosophy.'

The history of Western philosophy is often broken into four periods: ancient philosophy, medieval philosophy, modern philosophy, and contemporary philosophy. Western philosophy is generally accepted to begin in Greece around the year 580 B.C. and ancient Greek philosophy hits its zenith with the great Athenian philosophers Socrates (469–399 B.C.), Plato (427–347 B.C.), and Aristotle (384–322 B.C.). The era of ancient philosophy begins with the ancient Greeks and ends with the fall of the Roman Empire (around 401 A.D.)

The era of medieval philosophy begins with the fall of Rome and the eventual spread of Christianity through Europe. The most influential of these thinkers were the great theologians and Saints of the Roman Catholic Church Augustine (354–430), Anselm (1033–1109), and Thomas Aquinas (1225–1274). Augustine along with many other early Christian thinkers can be characterized as neo-Platonists; they attempted to meld Plato's work with Christian doctrine to create a coherent philosophical system. During much of the early medieval period the works of Aristotle are almost unavailable to the non-Arabic world. When Aristotle's works are introduced to Europe from the Arab world a new synthesis becomes available, and in the hands of Aquinas it becomes a powerful force. As Daniel Kolak and Garrett Thomson note in their book *The Longman Standard History of Philosophy*, the work of Aquinas 'can be regarded as an attempt to adapt the teachings of the Church to those of Aristotle, and in the process Aquinas defined a new Christian doctrine, which in many ways dominated medieval European thought.'[1]

It should be noted that during much of the medieval era most of the population of Europe was poorly educated and often illiterate, and that the main access to education was through the Church. Thus, the Church and its theologians controlled the education available to most of those lucky individuals who had any access to education at all. Before the invention of the printing press in 1455 the process of producing books was laborious; books had to be copied by hand by skilled craftsmen. Since it could take many months to copy a book, they were very expensive. Access to books came to those who were wealthy or had access to the Church's libraries. Thus, even if one had a desire to learn, and for poor peasants there would be little incentive to do so, access to education, for all practical purposes, came through the church. It is only after 1517 when Martin Luther (1483–1546) rebelled against the church in Germany that there was any organized resistance to Church dogma.

The division of the philosophical world into two periods prior to 1600 is not controversial. There is also little controversy about the labeling of the period following 1900 as the contemporary era. It remains problematic, however, what we should do with the nineteenth century and, in particular, John Stuart Mill. Some authors, such as the previously mentioned Kolak and Thomson, create a fifth category, namely, nineteenth-century philosophy. Others, such as Louis Pojman in his *Classics of Philosophy*, simply run modern philosophy through 1900.[2] In the case of Mill, there are arguments for either approach. Mill is very much a modern and, as we shall see, finds himself in agreement with many ideas which can be traced back to the philosophers and other intellectuals of the seventeenth and eighteenth century. However, Mill is rejecting some ideas and significantly changing others in ways that suggest his philosophy as a response to the modern era. It might be best to view Mill as a transitional figure that bridges the gap between the modern and contemporary era. But to see this we need to see how the moderns broke with the medieval philosophers, and to what extent Mill finds himself in agreement with the moderns' criticism of medieval philosophy and its methodology.

Perhaps the clearest and most succinct summary of the project shared by the modern philosophers is offered by Forrest E. Baird and Walter Kaufman in their book *From Plato to Derrida:*

> To a large extent, modern philosophy begins with a rejection of tradition. Whereas medieval philosopher such as Thomas Aquinas had taken great pains to incorporate and reconcile ancient writings, early modern philosophers such as Rene Descartes encouraged their readers to make a clean sweep of the past. Previous thinkers had been deluded by errors in thinking or had relied to heavily on authority. In the modern age, the wisdom of the past was to be discarded as error prone.[3]

As noted earlier, the medieval philosophers relied heavily upon authoritative figures and authoritative texts of the past. This did not sit well in the modern era. With the dawn of science in full view around them, the modern philosophers were looking for new tools to justify our beliefs about the world. Of course, the science of the 1600s was hardly the science that we have today. Yet, there are roots in the moderns' approach to philosophy that explicitly makes the scientific project possible. Galileo (1564–1642) was ordered by the Church in 1616 to neither advocate nor teach the radical suggestion that the earth rotates around the sun rather than vice versa. Galileo's telescopic observations were at odds with Church dogma, since Copernicus' heliocentric account is contrary to the geocentric account found in the Christian theology of the Church with its interpretation of scripture, and the physics of Aristotle. Thus, the Church's use of Christian theology and Aristotelian physics was an impediment to modern experimental science.

It was clear then that if science was to develop, new methods of investigation would be needed to replace authority figures and authoritative texts. As Baird and Kaufman put it: 'In the modern age, the wisdom of the past was to be discarded as error prone.'[4]

Rene Descartes (1596–1650) is often considered the father of modern philosophy. Descartes' influential *Meditations on First Philosophy* (1641) can be read as the first modern assault on the use of authority. As Descartes notes in the first paragraph of his first Meditation:

> Some years ago I was struck by the large number of falsehoods that I had accepted as true in my childhood, and by the highly doubtful nature of the whole edifice that I had subsequently based on them. I realized that it was necessary, once in the course of my life, to demolish everything completely and start again right from foundations if I wanted to establish anything at all in the sciences that was stable and likely to last.[5]

Medieval philosophy, according to the moderns, is insufficient in two important ways. The medieval account and its reliance on authority is error prone and offers an insufficient basis for experimental science. As Kolak and Thomson note:

> Up to the late sixteenth century, investigation consisted in studying authoritative texts such as those of Aquinas and the Bible, and debate comprised citing and making deductions from them. However, the new sciences, such as astronomy, had no place for arguments from authority. They relied on observation and reasoning. The English Philosopher Francis bacon strongly attacked authoritarian arguments on the grounds that the new science required freedom from the old traditions to investigate the universe without prejudice and superstition.[6]

The question then arises: If the moderns wish to reject medieval philosophy, what do they offer in its place? The answer will ultimately be a new approach to how we view the world, and our place in it that makes room for the new science, and, as we shall see, new approaches to politics and ethics as well.[7]

ii. METAPHYSICS AND EPISTEMOLOGY

There are various ways that one can be introduced to the study of philosophy. I have already discussed a historical approach above. But it is also possible to break philosophy down into four distinct subject matters or sets of questions the philosophers are interested in solving. Traditionally these four areas of study are metaphysics, epistemology, value theory, and logic. Here my discussion will follow that of Louis P. Pojman in his *Introduction to Philosophy: Classical and Contemporary Readings*.

Metaphysics is the branch of philosophy that discusses the nature of reality. Metaphysical questions include: What is ultimately real? Is reality made of one thing (e.g., matter) or is it made of something else (e.g., ideas, mind or spirit) or is it made of some combination of these or something else? Is there free will? Is there human nature? Is there a God? What is a person and does that thing persist through time? Do human beings survive death? If human beings are both minds and matter, how are these connected?

Epistemology is the branch of philosophy that discusses the nature of knowledge. The connection to metaphysics is immediate. Once one is presented with a metaphysical claim such as 'God exists,' the easy rejoinder is: How do you know that? And what exactly does it mean to know something? What is knowledge? Can I really know anything? Is it possible that I am wrong about all my beliefs and must be skeptical of all knowledge claims? What does it mean to say that something is true, and how could I justify such an assertion? As we saw above for the medieval philosophers, one approach to epistemology is to use authority figures and authoritative texts. The medieval philosopher can say that believe in some metaphysical claim is believable because Aquinas and scripture say so, and this is sufficient epistemological justification. But with the rejection of authority the moderns must look elsewhere.

Value theory (sometimes called axiology) is the branch of philosophy that discusses the nature of value. What makes something valuable? What is beauty? What is art? What is justice? What would a just society look like? What makes an action right or wrong? Are moral principles universally valid or do they depend on specific times, places, and cultural circumstances? Are there human rights? Are there natural human rights? Do rights and morality depend on religion? Once again, the medieval philosopher has an easier initial go of it, and the modern rejection of authority forces the modern philosopher to seek new justification.

Logic is the branch of philosophy that discusses the nature of arguments. What is a good argument? How can logic and good arguments support our metaphysical, epistemological, and value claims? Can our beliefs in deduction and induction be justified? What is a logical fallacy, and how can we tell when our arguments are unsuccessful? As we shall see, there are problems here for the moderns as well.[8]

As Pojman also notes, philosophy can also be studied in 'secondary areas' that work on 'conceptual and/or theoretical problems' that arise in other disciplines. So, for example, it is common to see university courses entitled 'Philosophy of X' where X could be science, law, economics, mathematics, art, language, etc. I even have a colleague who offers a course entitled 'Philosophy of the Emotions.' And it is common today to see courses in all three approaches offered in universities. Thus, courses such as 'Modern Philosophy,' 'Metaphysics,' and 'Philosophy of Science' are commonly offered.

So far my presentation of philosophy as it is practiced in the West has emphasized historical eras, the four traditional major areas, and the study of secondary areas. This multi-barreled approach is in my opinion necessary for a proper understanding of virtually any important thinker. Every important thinker is grounded in a particular era, has an approach to answering the questions raised by the four major areas, and has interests in specific secondary areas. But in the case of Mill it is essential. This is because Mill is a systematic philosopher. Mill is in two important ways a systematic philosopher. The seventeenth and eighteenth centuries produced several new approaches to philosophy and these new approaches are quite fruitful in the support of disciplines unheard of before the Modern era. Before the birth of Descartes there were those engaged in the study of what was then called 'natural philosophy,' but by Mill's lifetime we have clearly recognizable disciplines of physics, chemistry, and biology. Prior to the nineteenth century there were what was called 'philosophy of mind' and 'political economy,' but after Mill's death new disciplines such as psychology and economics are in something close to their modern forms. The economist Thomas Sowell is at best a lukewarm supporter of Mill. But in his *On Classical Economics* Sowell writes:

> Mill's contributions to economics considerably exceed those particular analyses in which he can be regarded as truly original. To have re-organized and presented as a structured whole the broad sweep of classical economics for the first time in his Principles of

> Political Economy was no small feat. Following in the wake of Ricardo's difficult to understand writings, Mill's making economics accessible to generations to come was a real service.[9]

Whether Mill was an original thinker in the area of economics or a mere presenter of the ideas of others is a question which I will return to momentarily, but there is no doubt that Mill found the discipline of political economy a disorganized mess. His *Principles of Political Economy* was the first work that presented economics as a system. It became the chief vehicle for teaching economics in universities for almost the next fifty years. Mill's *Principles* had no serious competitor until Alfred Marshall's *Principles of Economics* (1890). Although Marshall's work included important advances made by economists in the years after Mill's death, Mill's *Principles* was still used in as a university text well into the twentieth century. On the one hand, Mill had a great gift for taking disparate sources and putting them together as a unified whole.

But on the other hand, Mill was a systematic thinker in another way as well. Timothy Robinson in his *Aristotle in Outline* discusses how he finds Aristotle to be a systematic philosopher. I find that this reasoning works for Mill as well. Robinson notes that while the word 'systematic' can mean various things, there is the sense that when one describes a philosopher as systematic, this suggests that 'ideas developed in one area of investigation, often find applications in other areas as well.'[10] Thus, the study of one area of Mill's philosophy is often enriched by seeing what is developed in other areas as well. One can read Mill's work on say, political economy, with profit, exposure to his views on metaphysics; psychology, ethics, and other areas of his thought can be quite enlightening. But more importantly, without some exposure to Mill's overall system, it is possible to walk away with a somewhat misleading Mill. Finally, as Robinson notes, there is profit to be garnered in looking at a systematic thinker just to see how a philosophic system holds together. Is the system internally consistent? Does it allow one to make greater sense of the world? Does it do so in ways that seem to be an improvement over its competitors? Even if one answers such questions negatively, it is clear that the exercise is of value for further philosophical exploration.[11]

John Skorupski, an important Mill scholar who will be discussed in greater detail later, argues in his introduction to the *Cambridge*

Companion to Mill a similar point. Comparing Mill with Aristotle and the influential nineteenth century German philosopher Hegel, he suggests that these philosophers were all 'synthesizers whose influence depended on their wholeness and many sidedness.' Skorupski concludes that as Aristotle served this purpose for Athenian aristocrats, and Hegel served it for Prussian constitutionalists, so did Mill for humanist European liberals.[12]

iii. BRITISH EMPIRICISM

As noted above, much of Mill is clearly grounded in the modern philosophy of the seventeenth and eighteenth century. Later we shall see that Mill was influenced by critics of this worldview as well. It is for this reason that Skorupski has called Mill a 'late-modern thinker.'[13] But where some of the critics of this worldview ended up rejecting it completely, Mill wished to retain many of the insights that the modern philosophers of the seventeenth and eighteenth century had. In particular, while the mature John Stuart Mill broke company in important ways with his father, James Mill (1773–1836), and his father's mentor, Jeremy Bentham (1748–1832), he retained significant portions of their philosophies and intellectual views as well. One of the elements that remained was his thorough-going empiricist outlook, particularly in the areas of morals and politics. Students first coming to Mill may wonder why he constantly rejects 'innate' or 'intuitionist' approaches to morality or politics, but this is simply part of the empiricist tradition that he inherited from his father and Bentham. Ultimately, one can trace this inheritance back to the first great British Empiricist John Locke (1632–1704). But to help understand what Locke and the empiricist view contributes to the views of Bentham and the Mills, we need to flesh out this worldview in greater detail.

The modern philosophical world is often divided into two camps: The British Empiricists and the Continental Rationalists (the empiricists tended to be born and educated in the English speaking British Isles and the rationalists tended to be born and educated on the continent (e.g., Descartes in France)). It should be noted that the terms 'empiricist' and 'rationalist' were coined in a later era, and were certainly not used by these thinkers to describe themselves (e.g., John Locke, one of the early advocates for empiricism, was a trained medical professional, receiving a medical license from Oxford in 1675, and during his lifetime the term 'empiricist' referred to a discredited form of medical quackery). What the rationalists and empiricists shared was a rejection of the scholastic method of investigation of the world. What they disagreed about was the proper foundation for knowledge.

To state a complicated matter in as simple a way as possible, the empiricists believe that all knowledge is derived from the senses. It is from experience of the world that we gain knowledge about the world. On the other hand, the rationalists believe that there is at least some source of knowledge other than that derived from sense data. According to the rationalists, human reason is an important, perhaps the only, reliable source of information. Kolak and Thomson give a rather strong definition stating:

> Rationalism is roughly the view that reason, without the aid of sense perception, can give us knowledge of the world. Reason can discover self-evident axioms that govern the universe, and, in principle, all other knowledge can be deduced rationally from these axioms . . .[14]

Rationalism found its first major voice with Descartes. Locke is usually considered the first of the major British Empiricists. His two most influential works are *An Essay Concerning Human Understanding*, and *Two Treatises on Government*. Locke began work on the *Essay* in 1671, finished it in 1687, and first published it in 1690. The *Treatises* was first published in 1689. The *Essay* was Locke's major contribution to empiricist epistemology, and particularly Locke's *Second Treatise* is considered a classic of political liberalism. 'Political liberalism' or alternatively 'classical liberalism' and Locke's contributions to this worldview will be discussed in a later chapter. For now, we will concentrate on Locke's epistemological project. It may prove useful for the purpose of discerning the differences between the rationalist and empiricist perspective to compare Locke's epistemological views with that of the rationalist epistemology of Descartes. Descartes believed that we could without experience of the world come to the conclusion that 'clear and distinct ideas are true.' It is subject to philosophical debate whether Descartes' *Meditations* offers a sound rationalist justification for this claim. Philosophers call knowledge that is derived prior to experience a priori. In any case, Locke rejects this claim and Descartes' method for justifying it, because he believes that all knowledge is a posteriori, or derived after experience of the world. Louis Pojman puts it thus:

> Locke's work in the theory of knowledge is the first systematic assault on Cartesian [Descartes'] rationalism, the view that reason alone guarantees knowledge. Locke argued that if our claims to knowledge make any sense, they must be derived from the world. He rejects the rationalist notion that we have innate ideas (actual knowledge of metaphysical truths, such as mathematical truths, universals, and the laws of nature) . . .[15]

I will devote some time to Locke's rejection of innate ideas, because it is central to understanding many of Mill's moral arguments. As Locke and the empiricists see it, moral claims cannot be justified on the basis that they are self-evident, a priori, or founded on our deepest intuitions. Rather moral knowledge, like all other knowledge of the world, is based on experience in the world, and moral claims can and must be argued for on an experiential basis. Moral truths are not innate ideas, because there are no innate ideas. And Locke argues that often what often passes as an innate truth is merely what we as social beings have been taught by our culture to be true. Book I of Locke's *Essay* is an extended argument for rejecting the concept of innate ideas. Locke begins by discussing why many believe that there are such truths. He writes:

> There is nothing more commonly taken for granted than that there are certain principles, both speculative and practical (for they speak of both), universally agreed upon by all mankind: which therefore, they argue, must needs be the constant impressions which the souls of men receive in their first beings, and which they bring into the world with them, as necessarily and really as they do any of their inherent faculties.[16]

Locke suggests here that many believe that there are truths about the world that are universally accepted, and because these folks believe that everyone recognizes them, they must be innate ideas. But this is not necessarily true. It might be that we all experience the world in a similar manner, and that this would be the basis for such beliefs. If this were true then our universal truths are learned and not innately given. But Locke is unconvinced that there are any universal truths that all humans know. First, he will wish to argue that even if there were universal consent to these purported truths that does not prove that these ideas are innate.

> This argument, drawn from universal consent, has this misfortune in it, that if it were true in matter of fact, that there were certain truths wherein all mankind agreed, it would not prove them innate, if there can be any other way shown how men may come to that universal agreement, in the things they do consent in, which I presume may be done.[17]

It could be the case that there are truths which all human beings are justified in believing. But if this is the case, it is not because they are innate. Rather, as noted above, we all have experience of the same world. Thus, universal acceptance of some ideas will not justify the belief in innate ideas. But Locke goes on to note, those 'truths' that are usually offered as self-evident innate truths are not universally accepted.

> But, which is worse, this argument of universal consent, which is made use of to prove innate principles, seems to me a demonstration that there are none such: because there are none to which all mankind give an universal assent. I shall begin with the speculative, and instance in those magnified principles of demonstration, 'Whatsoever is, is,' and 'It is impossible for the same thing to be and not to be'; which, of all others, I think have the most allowed title to innate. These have so settled a reputation of maxims universally received, that it will no doubt be thought strange if any one should seem to question it. But yet I take liberty to say, that these propositions are so far from having an universal assent, that there are a great part of mankind to whom they are not so much as known.[18]

Locke's point here is even if there are laws of logic that all reasonable people should agree to, most people in the world nave not studied formal logic. Nowadays, it is possible to make Locke's point with greater force. Let's take Locke's second example which is sometimes called the law of non-contradiction, namely, that a proposition and its opposite cannot be true. So, in classical bimodal logics where there are only two truth values – true and false – if a proposition A is true, then not A must be false. But as John Nolt pointed out in his book *Logics*, the twentieth century saw the development of non-classical logics. By the way, 'logics' here is not a typographical error. Logicians have developed alternatives to classical logic, much as mathematicians have developed alternatives to Euclidian geometry. We now have logics such as infinite valued and fuzzy logics where there are far more than two truth values. So is the law of non-contradiction true? Is it true that two parallel lines never intersect? The answers depend on which logic or geometry you are using. Nolt makes the point rather succinctly: 'Is there a uniquely true logic? This book's answer, obviously, is no.'[19] If this is the case, then there are no laws of logic that would count as universal truths let alone innate universal truths.

Furthermore, even if there were a consensus on this issue, and most people agreed to accept the laws of a particular logic, there would still be according to Locke exceptions that would show that these ideas are not innate. Locke writes:

> For, first, it is evident, that all children and idiots have not the least apprehension or thought of them. And the want of that is enough to destroy that universal assent which must needs be the necessary concomitant of all innate truths: it seeming to me near a contradiction to say, that there are truths imprinted on the soul, which it perceives or understands not . . . If therefore these two propositions, 'Whatsoever is, is,' and 'It is impossible for the same thing to be and not to be,' are by nature imprinted, children cannot be ignorant of them: infants, and all that have souls, must necessarily have them in their understandings, know the truth of them, and assent to it.[20]

Of course, Locke is correct as far as he is going here. It strikes me as implausible that children are born with knowledge of, say, the Pythagorean Theorem, or that all humans at all times are aware of it. Modern developmental psychologists sometimes claim that normal human beings are born with the capacity to learn certain truths. But in an important passage Locke makes clear why the rejection of innate truths is essential to the modern project as he sees it. The belief in innate truths is a defense of the status quo. Locke writes:

> When men have found some general propositions that could not be doubted of as soon as understood, it was, I know, a short and easy way to conclude them innate. This being once received, it eased the lazy from the pains of search, and stopped the inquiry of the doubtful concerning all that was once styled innate. And it was of no small advantage to those who affected to be masters and teachers, to make this the principle of principles, – that principles must not he questioned. For, having once established this tenet, – that there are innate principles, it put their followers upon a necessity of receiving some doctrines as such; which was to take them off from the use of their own reason and judgment, and put them on believing and taking them upon trust without further examination: in which posture of blind credulity, they might be more easily governed by, and made useful to some sort of men, who had the skill and office to principle and guide them. Nor is it a small power it gives one man over another, to have the authority to be the dictator of principles, and teacher of unquestionable truths; and to make a man swallow that for an innate principle which may serve to his purpose who teacheth them. Whereas had they examined the ways whereby men came to the knowledge of many universal truths, they would have found them to result in the minds of men from the being of things themselves, when duly considered; and that they were discovered by the application of those faculties that were fitted by nature to receive and judge of them, when duly employed about them.[21]

I find this passage to be of great importance because it connects intimately Locke's epistemological commitments with his moral and political ones. The belief in innate ideas allows the lazy to suspend all inquiry. After all, one does not need to argue for self-evidently true innate ideas, offer evidence for them, or show how they to a better job of explicating the world as we experience it than their competitors; they are simply known by the powers of reason. Similarly, if one challenges the truth of one of these innate truths, there can be no need for argument. After all, only a liar or an insane person could claim to doubt what is self-evidently true.

Thus the belief in innate ideas is a powerful tool for those who wish to stifle debate, and defend the interests of the powerful. If it is self-evidently clear that the king has a divine right to rule, that peasants are unable to manage their own affairs, that the Church is the source of all moral knowledge, then anyone attacking the status quo is not merely a political instigator, but a heretic who is attacking reason itself. And the ability to attack your political opponents as unreasonable is no 'small power it gives one man over another.' The claim that your positions are innate truths can, when used effectively, end all debate. Thus, in Locke's view, any progressive or reform-minded thinker must challenge this epistemology at its core. It is only when we are challenged to apply 'those faculties that were fitted by nature to receive and judge them' that truths about the world can be known.

In addition to Locke's views about innate ideas there is another aspect of his epistemology that is relevant to our understanding of the views of Bentham and the Mills. One important aspect of this view involves what is nowadays called the nature/nurture debate. Are you what you are because of your environment, or are you primarily formed by the genetic inheritance you have received from your parents? How one resolves this debate has important implications for many public policy issues. Do schools make children smart, or do smart children do well in school? If children are products of their environment, then spending large sums on education seems like a good investment. On the other hand, if children's capacity to learn is largely a product of their genetic inheritance, then spending large sums of money on the education of the less intelligent children is a waste of money. Now few contemporary theorists come down strongly on one or the other side of this debate. Our current conventional wisdom is that both genes and environment are important contributors to human personality. But Locke was clearly on the environmentalists' side of this debate. Pojman summarizes this aspect of Locke's epistemology thus:

> According to Locke, the mind at birth is a tabula rasa, a blank slate. It is like white paper, devoid of characteristics until it receives sense perception. All knowledge begins with sensory experience upon which the powers of the mind operate, developing complex ideas, abstractions, and the like. In place of the absolute certainty that the rationalists sought to find, Locke says that apart from the knowledge of the self, most of what we know we know in degrees of certainty derived from inductive generalization. For example, we see the sun rise every morning and infer

> that it is highly probable that it will rise tomorrow, but we cannot be absolutely certain.[22]

One can make three points from Pojman's summary. One, the mind is a blank slate. Our personalities are formed by our experience of the world. Once again, there are important moral and political implications for this view, and they will be discussed in greater detail as we examine the work of Bentham and Mills.

Two, we see here the beginning of a psychological theory which will eventually be known as associationism. According to Locke, all ideas are derived from experience. Complex ideas are formed through sensation and reflection. Although Locke's version of associationism is crude, its more sophisticated forms are traceable back to Locke. Associationism as a simple theory has its roots in Locke's *Essay*, and Locke introduced the term 'association of ideas' in the 4th edition of the *Essay* (1700). Associationism will later be made into a workable psychological system in the eighteenth century, through the work of David Hartley (1705–1757) and James Mill. Associationism will be discussed in more detail later in this chapter in the section on psychology.

Three, there is beginning with Locke a need for a logic that will justify inductive inference. This problem of induction was acute enough to lead some readers of the influential British Empiricist David Hume (1711–1776) to believe that empiricism, taken to its logical conclusion, leads to skepticism about knowledge of the physical world. Although there is no reason to believe that John Stuart Mill was motivated by Humian skepticism, his contributions to inductive logic are an important part of his legacy. Mill's contributions to logic and induction deserve to be discussed in greater detail. A preliminary discussion follows with Mill's contribution to social science to follow in a later chapter.

iv. LOGIC AND *A SYSTEM OF LOGIC*

John Stuart Mill's *A System of Logic* (1843) was the work that gained him fame during his era. Mill would later in his autobiography suggest that it was one of his two most important works, and possible the one for which he would be remembered. Daniel Robinson in his *An Intellectual History of Psychology* states that Mill's *Logic* was immediately successful and, through eight editions in his own lifetime, served as the handbook of the scientific community. Contemporary science continues to rely on Mill's 'methods,' and our own easy commitment to the hypotheticoinductive method can be attributed to the immediate hold the *System of Logic* took on the scientific mind. Not many scientists in the late nineteenth century read Galileo; all of them read Mill.[23]

In this section, I will not focus on Mill's contributions to psychology and the development of social science. This will be covered in later chapters. Rather, it is to discuss how his views on logic impact his epistemological commitments. John Skorupski's work *John Stuart Mill* is arguably the best single source on Mill's overall philosophy, covering a detailed account of Mill as a systematic thinker. Early in this work he tells us: 'The root of Mill's philosophical thought is thoroughgoing naturalism.'[24] But his explanation of the term 'naturalism' is brief, and probably only helpful to an audience of professional academics. However, in Skorupski's defense, I have found in my own teaching that this concept and the related term 'transcendentalism' are not easily defined or explicated. The clearest example to present these two concepts that I am aware of is found in Philip Kitcher's 'Mill, Mathematics and the Naturalist Tradition.' Kitcher describes 'transcendentalism' thus:

> One of these conceptions, which I shall call 'transcendentalism', believes that a central task of philosophy is to identify fundamental conditions on human thought, representation, or experience, and that this enterprise is to be carried out by special philosophical methods that yield knowledge quite independently of experience, or of the deliverances of the natural sciences. Prime examples of transcendentalist philosophy can be found in Kant, in Frege, and, in recent philosophy, in the writings of Michael Dummett.'[25]

In short, there is a special apparatus needed to answer the fundamental questions of metaphysics and epistemology, and this methodology is quite distinct from the methodology that scientists use to investigate the world. We will shortly see an example of transcendentalism in the philosophy of Immanuel Kant. Kitcher describes 'naturalism' thus:

> Opposed to transcendentalism is a quite different philosophical

> tradition, one that emphasizes the idea of human subjects as part of nature, refuses to believe that there are special sources of philosophical knowledge whose deliverances are foundational to, or independent of, the methods and claims of the natural sciences, and conceives the philosopher as an 'under-laborer', working cooperatively with scientists, artists, and makers of social policy on the problems that arise at particular moments in human history, endeavoring to shape more adequate visions of the world and our place in it. This conception of Philosophy is appropriately called 'naturalism'. It is found, I believe, in Aristotle, Locke, Hume, and Dewey, and its leading contemporary exponent is W.V. Quine. Mill is not only one of the most important naturalists in the history of philosophy, but also, perhaps, the most thoroughly consistent.[26]

Skorupski goes on to draw a clear distinction between Mill's naturalism and Kant's transcendentalism. Skorupski suggests that both Mill and Kant would agree on one fundamental principle. Namely, if we accept a thoroughly naturalistic description of human thought then there can be no a priori knowledge of the natural world: 'Any grounds for asserting a proposition that has real content must be empirical grounds.' If this is the case then an empiricist philosophy must be able to demonstrate these grounds or else empiricism is reduced to skepticism. So, if naturalism is true then we are forced to choose between empiricism and skepticism.[27] As noted above, it is Hume that first raised this problem for empiricism, and Hume is often read as if there is no possibility of knowledge about the real world.

v. HUME'S FORK

In his *Enquiry Concerning Human Understanding* (1748) Hume makes a distinction which is nowadays called Hume's Fork. Hume suggests that all meaningful propositions are either 'relations of ideas' or 'matters of fact.' Examples of relations of ideas include 'all bachelors are unmarried men' and '4 + 5 = 9'. As Hume puts it: 'propositions of this kind are discoverable by the mere operation of thought, without dependence on what is anywhere existent in the universe.' Relations of ideas are 'intuitively or demonstratively certain' and to deny the truth one is to assert a contradiction.

Contemporary philosophers use the term analytic propositions instead of Hume's relations of ideas, but both terms make the same point. Testing the truth of such propositions is a matter of analyzing whether the ideas have the proper relationship. 'All women are female' does and 'all women are male' does not.[28]

Examples of matters of fact are 'the pencil is six inches long' and 'the boulder weighs a ton.' Matters of fact 'are not ascertained in the same matter; nor is the evidence of their truth, however great, of a like nature of the foregoing.' Consider the comparison: 'All women are female' is true and 'all women are male' is false without any investigation of the world. But to ascertain the truth of the claims 'the pencil is six inches long' and 'the pencil is not six inches long' you need to measure the pencil. It may be the case that the pencil is six inches long, but that is a factual matter. There is no logical contradiction in claiming that the pencil is seven inches long. On the other hand, 'the triangle has four sides' is logically contradictory.[29]

Hume's Fork is often used as the starting point for the skeptical reading of Hume. One can use a three-step argument to show how Hume's Fork can lead to skepticism. First, lets us to consider the difference between the two following claims: 'Every effect has a cause' and 'every event has a cause.' From Hume's point of view, the first claim is trivially true relation of ideas. To call something an effect is by definition to say it has a cause. When you look up the word 'effect' in the dictionary, you get something like 'what is produced by a cause.'[30] But this is not true of the second claim. If one looks up the word 'event' in the dictionary, you get something similar to 'something that happens; an occurrence.'[31] There is no mention of any effect. Therefore, if 'every event has a cause' is true, it must be a matter of fact.

Second, when we ascertain the truth of a matter of fact, like 'the pencil is six inches long' it is because we can measure length. But causes do not seem to be the kind of thing that we can measure. Sense experience allows us to experience length and weight. But we do not have sense experience of causes. So, the claim that 'A is caused by B' let alone 'Every A is caused by a B' cannot be a matter of fact. Since 'A is caused by B' clearly cannot be a relation of ideas, there is no logical basis for believing any claim of this sort is a reasonable proposition.

Third, since we have no basis for beliefs of the form 'A is caused by B,' all we are entitled to believe is that there has been a correlation between A and B in the past, where event A seems to follow event B. But since we cannot justify our belief in causes, we cannot justify the belief that correlations we have seen in the past will justify the belief in causal relations that cause similar correlations in the future. This would be to rather viciously beg the question. Thus, the belief in the uniformity of nature is unjustified.[32]

vi. KANT'S COPERNICAN REVOLUTION

Immanuel Kant was impressed by Hume's skeptical argument. He thinks Hume's attack on metaphysics raises rather forcefully whether it is even possible to discuss metaphysics at all. At various points he puts the question this bluntly: How is metaphysics possible at all?

This question bothered Kant so much that he published nothing in the eleven years prior to his *Critique of Pure Reason* (1781). Because many of his critics found the *Critique* incomprehensible, he later published the supposedly simpler *Prolegomena to Any Future Metaphysics* (1783). It is in this work he explicitly ties the motivation for writing the *Critique* to Hume. Kant writes:

> Since the Essays of Locke and Leibniz, or rather since the origin of metaphysics so far as we know its history, nothing has ever happened which was more decisive to its fate than the attack made upon it by David Hume.[33]

Similarly in a few pages Kant states:

> I openly confess, the suggestion of David Hume was the very thing, which many years ago first interrupted my dogmatic slumber, and gave my investigations in the field of speculative philosophy quite a new direction.[34]

Thus, as Kant sees it, the refutation of Humian skepticism was the first step in establishing any foundation for metaphysical belief. Kant's project in the *Critique* is to provide a basis for speculative philosophy. Garrett Thomson in his *An Introduction to Modern Philosophy* lays out Kant's project in detail. Over the next few paragraphs I will follow Thomson's lead, along with the previously mentioned Pojman.

Thomson asks whether the possibility of having theoretical knowledge that somehow transcends or goes beyond human experience is real. Can we make theoretical or a priori claims about God's existence, whether the soul survives death, or the feasibility of the Big Bang Theory? Although we aspire to such knowledge, knowledge that goes beyond everyday experience, Kant finds such knowledge is impossible. But to make this claim, Kant must tell us the conditions under which a priori knowledge is possible. Kant begins by noting that it is the case that mathematics and natural science are possible, so the question becomes: How are they possible? Kant answers this question by stating that mathematics and science rest on what he terms synthetic a priori judgments.[35]

To understand this category of the synthetic a priori we must briefly return to Hume. Recall that Hume believes that all meaningful statements are either relations of ideas or matters of fact. However, Kant thinks that Hume is moving too quickly here, and must slow down to make a few distinctions. Kant agrees that there is a clear distinction between the a priori and the a posteriori. But Kant also believes we must make a distinction between what he calls the analytic and the synthetic. According to Kant, analytic claims are true when the predicate term is included in the subject term; there is no new knowledge in the predicate term. A trivial example would be: 'the red ball is red.' 'Every mother is a female' can be seen to be one once the sentence is broken down. 'Every mother is a female' is logically equivalent to 'every female parent is a female,' and in this case the predicate term 'female' is clearly contained in the subject term 'female parent.' Synthetic statements, on the other hand, are ones where there is new knowledge in the predicate term. In the statement 'the pencil is six inches long' the predicate term 'six inches long' is new information, since this information is not included in the general definition of a pencil.

Thus with these tools in place, we can now classify Hume's relations of ideas as Kant's analytic a priori, and Hume's matters of fact as Kant's synthetic a posteriori. Once again, Hume found the claim 'every event to be cause' to be neither a relation of ideas nor a matter of fact, so it becomes some sort of pseudo-statement. Kant agrees in part. If all meaningful statements were either analytic a priori or synthetic a posteriori, then the statement 'every event has a cause would be meaningless.' But Kant suggests that there is a third category to consider, and every event has a cause is a synthetic a priori truth.

Synthetic a priori truths serve an important function for Kant. They 'define the necessary conditions for experience.' So in the case we have been considering, every event must have a cause, since otherwise 'an uncaused event could not be experienced.' If our experience of the world lacked any structure or order, we would experience a jumble of confusion. If we lacked the conceptual apparatus to make sense of our experience, then knowledge of the world would be impossible. In short, Kant believes that knowledge 'requires the cooperation of both sensible intuitions and concepts.' For Kant, 'thoughts without content are empty,' and 'intuitions without concepts are blind.' On the one hand, without the synthetic a priori conceptual apparatus we would be blind; we could make no sense of our experience of the world. But on the other hand, without experience the content would be empty; there would be nothing to give structure and order.[36]

So, as Pojman notes, although Kant began his philosophical career as a rationalist, Hume convinced him that all 'knowledge begins with experience. But he concluded that Hume was in error in believing that all our knowledge 'arises from experience.' Despite the 'flamboyant speculation' that one finds in the rationalists they were correct in one important insight; namely, that there is 'something determinate in the mind' that makes human knowledge possible. At the core of Kant's system is the belief that the mind has an order or structure that empowers our thought in a way that it 'imposes interpretative categories on our experience.' Thus the empiricists were wrong to suggest that we experience the world directly, but rather through the 'constitutive categories of the mind.' In the Kantian secondary literature this is commonly called Kant's Copernican Revolution.[37]

> Until now we have assumed that all our knowledge must conform to objects. But every attempt to extend our knowledge of objects by establishing something in regard to them a priori, by means of concepts, have, on this assumption, ended in failure. Therefore, we must see whether we may have better success in our metaphysical task if we begin with the assumption that objects must conform to our knowledge. In this way we would have knowledge of objects a priori. We should then be preceding in

> the same ways as Copernicus in his revolutionary hypothesis. After he failed to make progress in explaining the movements of the heavenly bodies on the supposition that they all revolved around the observer, he decided to reverse the relationship, and make the observer revolve around the heavenly body, the sun, which was at rest. A similar experiment can be done in metaphysics with regard to the intuition of objects. If our intuition must conform to the constitution of the object, I do not see how we could know anything of the objects a priori, but if the object of sense must conform to the constitution of our faculty of intuition, then a priori knowledge is possible.[38]

Once again, the contrast with Hume is important. Hume believed that matters of fact were known a posteriori, and that only analytic truths are known a priori. Kant opposes this formulation, and claims that synthetic a priori truths are not simply possible, but necessary for metaphysical speculation. Kant tells us that 'though all our knowledge begins with experience, it does not follow that it all arises out of experience.' In fact finds most of our mathematical truth to be synthetic; where Hume thought a mathematical truth such as '5 + 7 = 12' was a relation of idea, an analytic a priori truth, Kant thought that the predicate in this kind of case contains something not in the subject, and thus it is a synthetic a priori truth. Similarly our knowledge of time, space causality and the moral law are synthetic a priori truths as well.[39]

vii. REJECTING A PRIORI KNOWLEDGE

Thus, Kant's 'transcendental idealism' is one answer to Humian skepticism. But Skorupski notes that there is an interesting point of agreement between Kant and Mill. Both would conclude that if the human mind is merely a part of nature, then no knowledge of the world can be a priori. Then the question becomes: can there be a posteriori knowledge of the world grounded solely on our experience? Do we need transcendent ideas to ground our beliefs about the world, or can they be grounded in a naturalistic explanation? Mill's *System of Logic* attempts to answer these questions from an empiricist and naturalist perspective.[40] In his autobiography Mill explains the purpose of writing his Logic as follows:

> I have never indulged the illusion that the book had made any considerable impression on philosophical opinion. The German, or à priori view of human knowledge, and of the knowing faculties, is likely for some time longer (though it may be hoped in a diminishing degree) to predominate among those who occupy themselves with such inquiries, both here and on the Continent. But the 'System of Logic' supplies what was much wanted, a text-book of the opposite doctrine – that which derives all knowledge from experience, and all moral and intellectual qualities principally from the direction given to the associations.[41]

Here is a clear and unequivocal statement of purpose for Mill's *System of Logic*. Both the rationalists and Kant's theory of knowledge require a priori elements. Instead Mill offers a philosophical system that makes no appeal to the a priori. Echoing arguments that Locke made earlier in his attack on innate ideas, Mill argues that a priori knowledge is a false tool used to defend prejudices that cannot be justified with empirical evidence.

> I make as humble an estimate as anybody of what either an analysis of logical processes, or any possible canons of evidence, can do by themselves, towards guiding or rectifying the operations of the understanding. Combined with other requisites, I certainly do think them of great use; but whatever may be the practical value of a true philosophy of these matters, it is hardly possible to exaggerate the mischiefs of a false one. The notion that truths external to the mind may be known by intuition or consciousness, independently of observation and experience, is, I am persuaded, in these times, the great intellectual support of false doctrines and bad institutions.[42]

Recall that the American Civil War was fought from 1861–1865, and Abraham Lincoln signed the Emancipation Proclamation freeing the slaves in the Southern states in 1863; this is roughly twenty years after the first publication of the *System of Logic* in 1843. It is Mill's view that it is only through an unjustified reliance on 'moral intuitions' that the beliefs in African inferiority and the moral rightness of slavery can be maintained. During Mill's life there were calls for equal rights to women in England and the United States, and serious attempts to extend voting rights to women were undertaken. These efforts to extend the franchise to women would fail during Mill's lifetime, but as we will see in subsequent chapters the belief in the equality of women and a belief in equal rights for women was an important part of Mill's political agenda. But the point for our discussion here is that Mill believes that what stalls racial and gender justice in his era, is what still stalls efforts for civil rights today; the believe that we can put our faith in moral principles that somehow lie beyond human experience and empirical evidence.

> By the aid of this theory, every inveterate belief and every intense feeling, of which the origin is not remembered, is enabled to dispense with the obligation of justifying itself by reason, and is erected into its own all-sufficient voucher and justification. There never was such an instrument devised for consecrating all deep-seated prejudices. And the chief strength of this false philosophy in morals, politics, and religion, lies in the appeal which it is accustomed to make to the evidence of mathematics and of the cognate branches of physical science. To expel it from these, is to drive it from its stronghold: and because this had never been effectually done, the intuitive school, even after what my father had written in his Analysis of the Mind, had in appearance, and as far as published writings were concerned, on the whole the best of the argument. In attempting to clear up the real nature of the evidence of mathematical and physical truths, the 'System of Logic' met the intuitive philosophers on ground on which they had previously been deemed unassailable; and gave its own explanation, from experience and association, of that peculiar character of what are called necessary truths, which is adduced as proof that their evidence must come from a deeper source than experience.[43]

My guess is that 90% of those who wish to read Mill today will not need to grasp much more of Mill's *Logic* than what he has expressed in the last few passages. In offering his own radical version of naturalism and empiricism, he wishes to offer an alternative to Kant and the other a priori schools of human knowledge. By suggesting that even mathematics, logic, and the natural sciences can be grounded in what Quine would later call a naturalized epistemology (and I do not wish to suggest that there are not significant differences between Mill and Quine), Mill removes the need for the elaborate systems advocated by the German metaphysicians of the eighteenth and the nineteenth century. Morality and politics can rest on a system that derives all knowledge from experience, and all moral and intellectual principally from associationist psychology. If the intuitive philosophers can be bested in their areas of greatest strength, namely, mathematics and physics, then James Mill's *Analysis of the Phenomena of the Human Mind* becomes a satisfactory rebuttal of the intuitionist school of psychology.

The key element in Mill's radical epistemology was to reject a priori knowledge altogether. As J.B. Schneewind argues persuasively, Mill's *System of Logic* was not neutral in regard to moral and epistemological issues. Rather, at its core, it was the 'first major installment of his comprehensive restatement' of his empiricist epistemology and utilitarian ethics. It starts with an attack on 'intuitionism' arguing that societies should govern their conduct based upon scientific knowledge and not on 'authority, custom, revelation, or prescription.' The core question at the heart of the logic is the nature of inferential knowledge and the rules that govern such inferences. He argues that although deductive inferences are not entirely useless but they are not a source of new knowledge. Mill argues that deductions are actually arguments from particulars to particulars. So, the standard example used in logic:

Premise: All men are mortal
Premise: Socrates is a man
Conclusion: Socrates is mortal

We are entitled to the first premise because we are aware of many people, who resemble Socrates in the relevant aspects, have died in the past. Even in the case of geometrical knowledge the axioms of geometry are 'grounded on observations and are generalizations of what we have always experienced.' If we can develop the laws of psychology sufficiently, we can use them and human experience to justify what others call intuitive truth. Even the fact that humans of some era may find some truths of mathematics undeniable, undeniability is a psychological phenomena; it may be intuitively true that the shortest distance between two points is a straight line, but modern physics tells us this is not true for light traveling through space.

Mill ultimately believes that it is through experimentation and inductive generalizations that we gain knowledge about the world. While the Humian skeptic calls inductive generalizations into doubt and denies that they offer support for the believe that what has happened in the past will happen in the future, Mill believes that we do not need absolute certainty in these matters to ground the physical, social, and moral sciences. As Schneewind suggests:

> Science does not rely upon induction and experiment alone. It is only infrequently, Mill thought, that we will find genuine causal laws, that is, absolutely invariable sequences. More frequently we will find regularities which hold as far a limited experience shows but which, we have reason to believe, might well not hold under other quite different circumstances . . . This makes clear the aim of science: to discover the laws of nature and empirical laws, and to connect them . . . in such a way as to show how the unrestricted laws would give rise to the regularities reported by the empirical laws.

Thus, science advances as the regularities that are given to us by experience and association come closer to the laws of nature. This makes our science distinct in important ways from the laws of nature, since our regularities are approximations of the laws of nature.[44]

Mill ultimately never took Humian skepticism seriously. Partly, this was for historical reasons; Hume was out of fashion in England during much of Mill's life, and it was only with the republication of Hume's work after Mill's death, that interest in Hume was revived in the British Isles. But the philosophical reason for rejecting skepticism out of hand is Mill's commitment to a naturalized epistemology. Clearly, we experience certain regularities in the course of our lives. As a naturalist, the job is not so much to justify our belief that there are such regularities, but to figure out which ones have been established as essentially correct, and then help us further ground our scientific theories. The issue is to explain how such regularities work, not that they do work. Can regularities that we experience in nature be formulated as inductive generalizations that can produce useful approximations of the laws of nature? I throw coins in the air for a while and they keep falling to the earth, so I conclude that coins fall to the earth. I throw stones into the air for a while and conclude that stones fall to the earth. The brute facts are as they are; the job, once again, is to subsume such inductive generalizations under theories that approximate the laws of nature. There is an element of falliblism here; at any given time scientists may be mistaken in their inductive generalizations. But this is usually considered a strong point of modern science. Scientific theories are not mere dogma, since they have been subject to testing that would show them false. And if further testing did show them false, they would be subject to revision. Mill uses the example of meteorology to make this point, although admittedly in a slightly different context. Mill writes:

> Any facts are fitted, in themselves, to be a subject of science which follow one another according to constant laws, although those laws may not have been discovered, nor even be discoverable by our existing resources. Take, for instance, the most familiar class of meteorological phenomena, those of rain and sunshine. Scientific inquiry has not yet succeeded in ascertaining the order of antecedence and consequence among these phenomena, so as to be able, at least in our regions of the earth, to predict them with certainty, or even with any high degree of probability. Yet no one doubts that the phenomena depend on laws, and that these must be derivative laws resulting from known ultimate laws, those of heat, electricity, vaporization, and elastic fluids. Nor can it be doubted that if we were acquainted with all the antecedent circumstances, we could, even from those more general laws, predict (saving difficulties of calculation) the state of the weather at any future time. Meteorology, therefore, not only has in itself every natural requisite for being, but actually is, a science; though, from the difficulty of observing the facts on which the phenomena depend (a difficulty inherent in the peculiar nature of those phenomena), the science is extremely imperfect; and were it perfect, might probably be of little avail in practice, since the data requisite for applying its principles to particular instances would rarely be procurable.[45]

But to explain the fact that we do experience such regularities is it necessary to appeal to Kantian transcendentalism? Mill thinks the associationist psychology that he was first introduced to by his father at an early age gives him everything he needs to base the naturalist account. It is to this that I now turn my attention. I will discuss the part of Mill's *System of Logic* that relates to the moral sciences in a later chapter.

viii. PSYCHOLOGY AND ASSOCIATIONISM

Associationist psychology can be traced back to Aristotle and Plato if one is inclined to do so. However, we are interested in the version that influenced Mill, and this associationist psychology is a primarily a product of modern era empiricism. In his *History of the Association Psychology* Howard Warren has this to say:

> The term association, as used by the English psychologists of the eighteenth and nineteenth centuries, applies primarily to the sequences that occur in trains of memory or imagination or thought: their problem was to formulate the principles involved in such sequences. According to the view generally adapted by these thinkers, one such experience follows another through certain definite relationships. Thus, one idea may serve to recall another which it resembles it or which was contiguous to it in former experience. Here we have the narrowest view of associationism, conceived as the principle by which trains of ideas are induced. Starting with this fundamental conception, the scope of the principle has been broadened in various directions.[46]

Just as we can find the origins of Mill's empiricism in the work of John Locke, we can trace elements of Mill's associationist psychology to Locke as well. In a previous section we looked closely at Locke's rejection of innate ideas, but Locke had a positive empiricist project as well. In other words, Locke argues that we should accept the empiricist account both because we should reject innate ideas and also because the empiricist account can be fully articulated. Locke called his approach to philosophy 'the new way of ideas.' An idea is whatever 'the mind perceives in itself or is the immediate object of perception, thought or understanding.'[47] Nowadays the term 'ideas' often means some fully articulated thoughts, but to Locke this term can simply mean some brute sort of experience. Locke writes:

> Every man being conscious to himself that he thinks; and that which his mind is applied about whilst thinking being the ideas

> that are there, it is past doubt that men have in their minds several ideas, such as are those expressed by the words whiteness, hardness, sweetness, thinking, motion, man, elephant, army, drunkenness, and others . . . Let us then suppose the mind to be, as we say, white paper, void of all characters, without any ideas: How comes it to be furnished . . . To this I answer, in one word, from EXPERIENCE. . . . And thus we come by those ideas we have of yellow, white, heat, cold, soft, hard, bitter, sweet, and all those which we call sensible qualities . . . This great source of most of the ideas we have . . . I call SENSATION. . . . Secondly, the other fountain from which experience furnisheth the understanding with ideas, is the perception of the operations of our own mind within us, as it is employed about the ideas it has got; which operations, when the soul comes to reflect on and consider, do furnish the understanding with another set of ideas, which could not be had from things without. And such are perception, thinking, doubting, believing, reasoning, knowing, willing, and all the different actings of our own minds . . . so I Call this REFLECTION . . .[48]

Once again, the mind at birth is a blank slate. It is through sensation and reflection that more complex ideas are formed through a process of association. Thus the mind is ultimately composed of brute sensations and reflections. These sensations and reflections he calls simple ideas. Although the details of Locke's project are not necessary for our purposes, simple ideas can be combined together to form more complex ideas, and as those more complex ideas are combined with other complex ideas sophisticated thought is possible. Locke's contribution to the birth of British associationist psychology is as follows:

> Some of our ideas have a natural correspondence and connexion one with another: it is the office and excellency of our reason to trace these, and hold them together in that union and correspondence which is founded in their peculiar beings. Besides this, there is another connexion of ideas wholly owing to chance or custom. Ideas that in themselves are not all of kin, come to be so united in some men's minds, that it is very hard to separate them; they always keep in company, and the one no sooner at any time comes into the understanding, but its associate appears

> with it; and if they are more than two which are thus united, the whole gang, always inseparable, show themselves together.[49]

Some small refinements were added to the theory by other early British Empiricists, but the next major step was proposed by the physician David Hartley (1705–1757). His major work *Observations on Man, His Frame, His Duty, and His Expectations* (1749) offered a physiology consistent with associationist psychology. As Schneewind has it, Hartley's major advancement was inspired by Isaac Newton (1643–1727) and a suggestion he made in his *Optics*. Hartley claimed that human consciousness could be explained by vibrations transmitted by way of nerves. Different sensations could provide different vibrations, or vibrations in a different location. Thus, Hartley offered a 'thoroughgoing attempt to provide a neurophysiological basis for the mental processes of sensation, imagery, and association.'[50]

ix. JAMES MILL AND ASSOCIATIONISM

James Mill was impressed with Hartley's work, and incorporated many of Hartley's ideas into his *Analysis of the Phenomena of the Human Mind* (1829). As Warren notes, James Mill's *Analysis* was the 'classic work of nineteenth century' associationist psychology, as much as Hartley's was the 'classic work of the eighteenth century.' Furthermore, the second edition of the *Analysis* in 1869 included additional commentary by the influential British philosopher and psychologist Alexander Bain and edited with substantial additional commentary by John Stuart Mill. As Warren sees it, the second edition of James Mill's analysis 'constitutes the most representative view of the association psychology.'[51]

James Mill is, of course, operating in the empiricist tradition of Locke and Hume. Thus, some of the details will seem familiar at this point. However, James Mill's summary of his position is succinct and clear. James Mill writes:

> We have now surveyed the simple and obvious phenomena of the mind. We have seen, first, that we have SENSATIONS; secondly, that we have IDEAS, the copies of those sensations; thirdly, that those ideas are sometimes SIMPLE, the copies of one sensation; sometimes COMPLEX, the copies of several sensations so

> combined as to appear not several ideas, but one idea; and, forthly, that we have TRAINS of those ideas, or one succeeding another without end.[52]

So, James Mill tells us these are the 'simple facts of our nature,' and they are 'attested by experience.'

James Mill also suggests that just like there are degrees in sensations and ideas there are also degrees in associations. Some associations can be said to be stronger than others. An association is stronger than another when:

> First, when it is more permanent than another: Secondly, when it is performed with more certainty: Thirdly, when it is performed with more facility.[53]

James Mill also suggests that there are two primary causes for the strength of associations: the 'vividness of the associated feeling' and the 'frequency of the association.'[54]

James Mill uses the following example to show how this works in practice. Consider the example of first learning to use a musical instrument. The repetition of practice seems to increase both the vividness and frequency of the associations involved. James Mill writes:

> At first, the learner, after thinking of each successive note, as it stands in his book, has each time to look out with care for the key or the string which he is to touch, and finger he is to touch with, and is every moment committing mistakes, Repetition is well known to be the only means of overcoming these difficulties. As the repetition goes on, the sight of the note, or even the idea of the note, becomes associated with the place of the key or string; and that of the key or the string with the proper finger. The association for a time is imperfect, but at last becomes so strong, that it is formed with the greatest rapidity, without an effort, and almost without consciousness.[55]

Thus, we find Mill on one side of a debate between English empiricism and the various French and German a priori schools. This debate continues today in the analytic philosophical tradition that has its roots in British empiricism and continental philosophic tradition that has its roots in Descartes and Kant along with other thinkers on the continent (i.e., not the British Isles). Robinson in his history of psychology mentioned above suggests that the same debate can also be found in the twentieth century psychology as well. It is perhaps the most important influence on the mature Mill's social, political, and ethical thought. I now turn to other influences on Mill.

CHAPTER 2

MILL'S EDUCATION AND EARLY INFLUENCES

i. JAMES MILL

As Bruce Mazlish tells us in his *James and John Stuart Mill*, there are not many good sources for James Mill's early life. James Mill wrote no autobiography, his letters have never been collected for publication, and there is only one contemporary biographical account by Alexander Bain in 1882. There are two main reasons for this. First, James Mill was born into less than wealthy circumstances; he only became well known in his middle age, and the parish of Logie Pert in Scotland, where he was born, had a population of roughly nine hundred. Records of his early life under these circumstances have not survived. Secondly, James Mill 'resolutely turned his back on the past' and did nothing to preserve the details of his youth. He was in many ways proud of being a 'self-made man' and gave the impression of having been 'practically sprung from his own loins.' However, the biography by Bain is a good one since 'Bain interviewed many of those who knew Mill during his youth, as well as during the course of his life' and Bain had access to some of James Mill's letters that have not survived.[1] My account over the next few paragraphs will rely on Mazlish, Bain, and Terrence Ball's 'James Mill.'

As noted above, apart from not leaving behind an autobiography, James Mill never wrote down any of the details of his early life, and even his son John had only a crude sketch of his father's early life. In his *Autobiography* John Stuart Mill wrote:

> I was born in London, on the 20th of May, 1806, and was the eldest son of James Mill, the author of the *History of British*

> *India*. My father, the son of a petty tradesman and (I believe) small farmer, at Northwater Bridge, in the county of Angus, was, when a boy, recommended by his abilities to the notice of Sir John Stuart, of Fettercairn, one of the Barons of the Exchequer in Scotland, and was, in consequence, sent to the University of Edinburgh at the expense of a fund established by Lady Jane Stuart (the wife of Sir John Stuart) and some other ladies for educating young men for the Scottish Church. He there went through the usual course of study, and was licensed as a Preacher, but never followed the profession; having satisfied himself that he could not believe the doctrines of that or any other Church. For a few years he was a private tutor in various families in Scotland, among others that of the Marquis of Tweeddale; but ended by taking up his residence in London, and devoting himself to authorship. Nor had he any other means of support until 1819, when he obtained an appointment in the India House.[2]

However we do know a little more than this. James Mill was born on 6 April 1773 at Northwater Bridge in the county of Forfarshire in the parish of Logie Pert in Scotland. This parish had a population of about nine hundred. His father, James Milne, was a shoemaker and small-farmer who is described by Ball as 'quiet, mild-mannered, and devout.' His mother, Isabel Fenton Milne, Ball describes as 'a more forceful figure.' Maizlish tells us that she had 'a legend of better times in her background' and that she was 'proud and even haughty.' Isabel had great ambitions for her first-born son, so she changed her husband's undistinguished name 'Milne' to the less common and more English-sounding 'Mill.'[3] As Ball notes Isabel 'kept young James away from other children, demanding that he spend most of his waking hours immersed in study.'[4] Bain tells us that James Mill 'neither assisted in his father's trade, nor took any part in the labour of the field . . . his own sole occupation was study.'[5] As Ball points out, James Mill was quite successful at this occupation. Ball writes:

> Before the age of seven he had shown a talent for elocution, composition, and arithmetic, as well as Latin and Greek. The local minister saw to it that James received special attention at the parish school. At age ten or eleven, he was sent to Montrose Academy . . . Mill was persuaded by the parish minister and his

> mother to study for the ministry. Mill's decision evidently pleased Lady Jane Stuart, wife of Sir John Stuart of Fettercairn, who headed a local charity founded for the purpose of educating poor but bright boys for the Presbyterian ministry. Mill, eminently qualified in both respects, became the recipient of Lady Jane's largesse. As it happened, she and Sir John were just then looking for a tutor for their fourteen-year old daughter Wilhelmina. They offered the job to James Mill; he accepted; and when the Stuart family moved to Edinburgh, he accompanied them.[6]

In 1790, at the age of eighteen, James Mill enrolled in the University of Edinburgh. By day he was a student in the university, at night he was a tutor to Wilhelmina. Ball tells us that the Scottish universities 'had earlier been the hub of the Scottish Enlightenment and were still the premier universities in Britain.' Mazlish tells us that while he was a student at the University of Edinburgh, James Mill 'took special training in divinity, while reading widely on his own in the secular authors of the Enlightenment.' He received his first degree in 1794, and by 1798 he was licensed as a preacher. However, he was unable to find a permanent position as a minister, and it was at this same time that he began to question his religious views. Mazlish writes:

> Finally, in 1802, approaching thirty and still unable to earn a living, Mill decided to seek his fortune outside barren Scotland. Sir John Stuart, off to attend his duties in Parliament, gave his protégé a seat to London in his carriage.[7]

James Mill had given up any interest in a religious profession, and instead decided to make a living as a public intellectual. This would have been impossible in Scotland, and not an easy life in London. Ball writes:

> From 1802 until his appointment as an assistant examiner of correspondence at the East India Company in 1819 Mill's literary labors were prodigious. Besides some 1,400 editorials, he wrote hundreds of substantial articles and reviews, as well as several books, including his *History of British India* in three large volumes. Although some of these were doubtless labors of love, most were labors of necessity, for Mill had to support himself

> and his wife Harriet, whom he married in 1805, and a fast-growing family. The first of his nine children, born in 1806, was named John Stuart in honor of his father's Scottish patron.[8]

It is interesting that James Mill, a lifelong advocate of birth control, would have nine children; particularly curious given his apparent disgust with his wife's intellect. A final oddity is that none of James Mill's sons would ever have children.

One more important detail of James Mill's life will be needed. Soon after the birth of his son John, James Mill befriended Jeremy Bentham. Ball describes their relationship as follows:

> In late 1807 or early 1808 James Mill met Jeremy Bentham, with whom he soon formed a political and philosophical alliance. The two were in some respects kindred spirits. Both wished and worked for religious toleration and legal reform; both favored freedom of speech and press; both feared that the failure to reform the British political system – by, among other things, eliminating rotten boroughs and extending the franchise – would give rise to reactionary intransigence on the one hand, and revolutionary excess on the other. But the two men were of vastly different temperaments and backgrounds. Bentham, a wealthy bachelor, was an eccentric genius and closet philosopher. The poor, harried and hard-working Mill was the more practical and worldly partner in that peculiar partnership . . . Despite their differences, Mill proved to be Bentham's most valuable ally. A better writer and abler advocate, Mill helped to make Bentham's ideas and schemes more palatable and popular than they might otherwise have been.[9]

Several aspects of James Mill's life have clear implications for decisions that directly influenced the early education of John Stuart Mill. First, James Mill lived in near poverty and under constant financial pressure well into his adult life. It was only after the publication of his *History of British India* and his subsequent employment at the East India Company that he had anything like financial security. At this point he was over 45. Secondly, although James Mill considered himself a self-made man, he was dependent for much of his life on wealthy sponsors; first the Stuarts and later Jeremy Bentham. During the years of his marriage his family spent a great deal of time in homes owned by the wealthy Bentham. Thirdly, James Mill was the product of a strict upbringing and a strenuous early education. He was a child prodigy, and as we shall see, so was Jeremy Bentham. Fourthly, James Mill was in today's language a workaholic. It is hard to underestimate the hours involved as an author in supporting a wife and nine children. This is especially true considering how radical many of James Mill's views were at the time and when we add in the hours he spent on his first-born son's education.

ii. JOHN STUART MILL'S EDUCATION

Those with little interest in philosophy or history often find the story of his education fascinating nonetheless. A recent biography of Mill sets it up as follows:

> John Stuart Mill was a test case for his father's and Bentham's theory that every person is born as a tabula rasa – a clean slate – whose mind is shaped entirely by his life experiences, especially those of childhood. Mill was raised in an intellectual Petrie dish, explicitly designed to produce an ideal standard-bearer for radicalism, rationalism and reform. Raised to be a 'worthy successor' to both his father and [Bentham] Mill was given a home education which has been a source of wonderment and condemnation ever since.[10]

Isaiah Berlin, the noted political philosopher and the theorist who popularized the terms 'positive and negative liberty,' called this educational experiment 'an appalling success.'[11]

In this section I will discuss the aspect of this 'appalling success' that was successful. In the next section I will discuss its defects. In his autobiography Mill writes that this education left him intellectually many years ahead of his peers. The education began early and rigorously. Mill writes:

> I have no remembrance of the time when I began to learn Greek. I have been told that it was when I was three years old. My earliest recollection on the subject, is that of committing to memory what my father termed Vocables, being lists of common Greek words, with their signification in English, which he wrote

> out for me on cards. Of grammar, until some years later, I learnt no more than the inflexions of the nouns and verbs, but, after a course of vocables, proceeded at once to translation; and I faintly remember going through Aesop's Fables, the first Greek book which I read.

Thus, lacking a standard English to Greek dictionary, Mill learned Greek by sitting at the table where his father worked and asking for the meaning of new words as they appeared. Mill was required to ask his father 'for the meaning of every word which I did not know.' By the time he was eight years old Mill recalled reading the:

> whole of Herodotus, and of Xenophon's *Cyropaedia* and *Memorials of Socrates*; some of the lives of the philosophers by Diogenes Laertius; part of Lucian, and Isocrates' *ad Demonicum* and *ad Nicoclem*. I also read, in 1813, the first six dialogues (in the common arrangement) of Plato, from the Euthyphron to the Theaetetus inclusive . . .

Mill recalls this education as so demanding that it included 'much that I could by no possibility have done.' But somehow Mill did it. Once again, even though James Mill was saddled with the task of publishing works to support his family while also writing the *History of British India*, he still was willing to extend significant energy to the education of his son. As Mill recalls it, his father 'the most impatient of men' was willing to allow this 'incessant interruption' of the elder Mill's work day. In the evenings, it was time to tutor his son in arithmetic.

But this was only a part of young Mill's studies. He recalls that much of his education was self-selected. He writes:

> Much of it consisted in the books I read by myself, and my father's discourses to me, chiefly during our walks. From 1810 to the end of 1813 we were living in Newington Green, then an almost rustic neighbourhood. My father's health required considerable and constant exercise, and he walked habitually before breakfast, generally in the green lanes towards Hornsey. In these walks I always accompanied him, and with my earliest recollections of green fields and wild flowers, is mingled that of the account I gave him daily of what I had read the day before.

Mill recalls this as largely a 'voluntary rather than prescribed exercise.' We can also see the dawning of Mill's lifelong interest in botany. Mill would take notes on his daily reading, and read them to his father during their walks. His chief interest at the time appeared to be history. He recalls reading histories by Robertson, Hume, and Gibbon. He took great delight in Watson's *Philip the Second and Third* and Hooke's *History of Rome*. He also recalls reading 'the first two or three volumes of a translation of Rollin's *Ancient History*, beginning with Philip of Macedon.' Langhorne's translation of Plutarch, Burnet's *History of his Own Time*, the historical part of the Annual Register, Millar's *Historical View of the English Government*, Mosheim's *Ecclesiastical History*, McCrie's *Life of John Knox*, and 'even Sewel's and Rutty's *Histories of the Quakers*.'[12]

Mill also recalls that his father 'was fond of putting into my hands books which exhibited men of energy and resource in unusual circumstances, struggling against difficulties and overcoming them.' Of these Mill recalls Beaver's *African Memoranda* and 'Collins's *Account of the First Settlement of New South Wales*.' Books which Mill 'never wearied of reading' were *Anson's Voyage*, and a collection of 'Voyages . . . beginning with Drake and ending with Cook and Bougainville.' Mill had few children's books but recalls reading *Robinson Crusoe*. Although James Mill did not prevent his son from reading . . . 'books of amusement . . . he allowed them very sparingly.' James Mill owned few such works, but he borrowed several for his son. Mill remembers reading 'the *Arabian Nights*, Cazotte's *Arabian Tales, Don Quixote*, Miss Edgeworth's "*Popular Tales*," and a book of some reputation in its day, Brooke's *Fool of Quality*.'[13]

Latin was then added to the younger Mill's studies, but the major change in his duties was the requirement to take on the education of his siblings. Mill recalls this with mixed emotions. He writes:

> In my eighth year I commenced learning Latin, in conjunction with a younger sister, to whom I taught it as I went on, and who afterwards repeated the lessons to my father: and from this time, other sisters and brothers being successively added as pupils, a considerable part of my day's work consisted of this preparatory teaching. It was a part which I greatly disliked; the more so, as I was held responsible for the lessons of my pupils, in almost as full a sense as for my own: I however derived from this discipline the great advantage of learning more thoroughly and retaining

> more lastingly the things which I was set to teach: perhaps, too, the practice it afforded in explaining difficulties to others, may even at that age have been useful. In other respects, the experience of my boyhood is not favourable to the plan of teaching children by means of one another. The teaching, I am sure, is very inefficient as teaching, and I well knew that the relation between teacher and taught is not a good moral discipline to either.

The remainder of Mill's account of his education is no less amazing, but, perhaps at this point anticlimactic. Mill continues his reading of Plato, and like his father, will develop a lifelong love for Socrates and Plato; Mill's mature works are peppered with references to Socrates's character. He will read Aristotle and study scholastic logic. He will help edit James Mill's *History of British India*, and he will continue his walks with his father where the topic will change to political economy. The leading economic theorist at this time is David Ricardo who is a household guest and confidant of James Mill. Alexander Bain, in *John Stuart Mill: A Criticism with Personal Recollections*, points out that the account in the *Autobiography* actually understates Mill's efforts. Bain cites a letter written to Sir Samuel Bentham, the brother of Jeremy Bentham, in 1819 at age thirteen where more works are mentioned. Bain suggests that the 'enumeration' in the letter 'is much fuller than in the *Autobiography*,' and the 'account of the Higher Mathematics of this period is slightly deficient in the *Autobiography*' as well.[14]

I have gone into great detail here to make a few points. First, the amount and complexity of the books Mill recalls reading is simply amazing. This is a discussion of the education of a child before the age of twelve. David Hume's *History of England* alone runs to six long and dense volumes. Secondly, Mill's education was a classical education. He was fluent in Greek at an early age, and as we shall see, the influence of Ancient Greece never left him. Thirdly, James Mill and Bentham were looking for an heir to carry out the utilitarian revolution to the next generation. Mill was raised to do hard intellectual labor and to admire those who struggle against long odds. And his life attests to the fact that however taxing this education was, by and large it was a success. Mill writes:

> In the course of instruction which I have partially retraced, the point most superficially apparent is the great effort to give,

> during the years of childhood an amount of knowledge in what are considered the higher branches of education, which is seldom acquired (if acquired at all) until the age of manhood. The result of the experiment shows the ease with which this may be done, and places in a strong light the wretched waste of so many precious years as are spent in acquiring the modicum of Latin and Greek commonly taught to schoolboys; a waste, which has led so many educational reformers to entertain the ill-judged proposal of discarding these languages altogether from general education. If I had been by nature extremely quick of apprehension, or had possessed a very accurate and retentive memory or were of a remarkably active and energetic character, the trial would not be conclusive; but in all these natural gifts I am rather below than above par; what I could do, could assuredly be done by any boy or girl of average capacity and healthy physical constitution: and if I have accomplished anything, I owe it, among other fortunate circumstances, to the fact that through the early training bestowed on me by my father, I started, I may fairly say, with an advantage of a quarter of a century over my contemporaries.

At this point classical political economy – the forerunner to what we call economics today – was added to the picture. James Mill was a leading economic thinker of the time and introduced his son to the works of David Ricardo. And the basis of the economic work that Mill would write later in his life was largely Ricardian economics, which he learned well in long daily walks with his father. Mill writes:

> Though Ricardo's great work was already in print, no didactic treatise embodying its doctrines, in a manner fit for learners, had yet appeared. My father, therefore, commenced instructing me in the science by a sort of lectures, which he delivered to me in our walks. He expounded each day a portion of the subject, and I gave him next day a written account of it, which he made me rewrite over and over again until it was clear, precise, and tolerably complete. In this manner I went through the whole extent of the science; and the written outline of it which resulted from my daily compte rendu, served him afterwards as notes from which to write his *Elements of Political Economy*. After this I read Ricardo, giving an account daily of what I read, and discussing,

> in the best manner I could, the collateral points which offered themselves in our progress.

Once again Mill's education was not the passive education that one sees from too many schools today. The whole point of his father's lectures was to aid young Mill to be, once again, an active collaborator in his father's work.

Boyhood Trip to France

He was now sent to France to visit Bentham's brother, General Sir Samuel Bentham, for the purpose of learning French. Initially the trip was to last six months. Mill enjoyed himself so thoroughly in this far more normal environment that he managed to find excuses to delay his return, and the trip ended up lasting fourteen months. During this time he succeeded in learning French, and developed a lifelong love of France, French culture, and politics. He also developed what would become a lifelong interest in botany. But most importantly, the Bentham household was filled with love and affection, a quality that one would not ascribe to James Mill's. He returned home in July 1821, barely fifteen.

He has at this age become fluent in English, Greek, Latin, and French; become familiar with history, higher mathematics, economic theory, and psychology at levels that surpass a standard bachelor's degree in these disciplines; edited his father's *History of British India*, and written the outline for his father's *Elements of Political Economy*. For reasons that are far from clear, an early version of Bentham's *Principles of Morals and Legislation* was published in French, before it was published in English. Now fluent in French, Mill can now begin the study of Bentham.

iii. MILL'S INTRODUCTION TO BENTHAM

Although he grew up in a Benthamite household (his father and many of the family guests were largely in agreement with Bentham's philosophy), reading Bentham had an enormous impact on Mill. He writes:

> Yet in the first pages of Bentham it burst upon me with all the force of novelty. What thus impressed me was the chapter in

> which Bentham passed judgment on the common modes of reasoning in morals and legislation, deduced from phrases like 'law of nature,' 'right reason,' 'the moral sense,' 'natural rectitude,' and the like, and characterized them as dogmatism in disguise, imposing its sentiments upon others under cover of sounding expressions which convey no reason for the sentiment, but set up the sentiment as its own reason. It had not struck me before, that Bentham's principle put an end to all this. The feeling rushed upon me, that all previous moralists were superseded, and that here indeed was the commencement of a new era in thought. This impression was strengthened by the manner in which Bentham put into scientific form the application of the happiness principle to the morality of actions, by analysing the various classes and orders of their consequences. The feeling rushed upon me, that all previous moralists were superseded, and that here indeed was the commencement of a new era in thought . . . When I laid down the last volume of the Traité, I had become a different being. The 'principle of utility' understood as Bentham understood it, and applied in the manner in which he applied it through these three volumes, fell exactly into its place as the keystone which held together the detached and fragmentary component parts of my knowledge and beliefs. It gave unity to my conceptions of things. I now had opinions; a creed, a doctrine, a philosophy; in one among the best senses of the word, a religion.[15]

Mill would remain a solid Benthamite for the next ten years.

iv. THE EAST INDIA COMPANY

The publication of his father's *History of British India* in 1818 had a profound influence on Mill's life. The book was a surprising success, and James Mill was no longer an obscure writer, but a well-known authority on India. This led to James Mill being offered a position with the East India Company – a quasi governmental entity that ran British India – and the family no longer had to struggle financially. Mill followed his father into the company as an intern the day after his seventeenth birthday and would stay employed with the company for thirty-five years. He was head of the company when Parliament took it over in 1858 following the

Indian Mutiny of 1857; he was offered a position in the new entity, but declined, and retired on a substantial pension.

At the age of twenty-five Mill had a 'mental crisis' that he discusses in a chapter of his autobiography. Although Mill describes as if it were a mental breakdown, Bain and other contemporaries saw no change in his behavior. Probably the best way to understand this episode is as a loss of 'religious faith.' He became a fully-fledged Benthamite utilitarian at the age of fifteen, and left the 'church' at age twenty-five. What he converted to I will discuss in detail in Chapter 4. But most importantly, he never stopped being a utilitarian.

v. HARRIET TAYLOR

The last major influence on Mill's life occurred when he began what he would later describe in his autobiography as the 'most valuable friendship of his life.' He met Harriet Taylor, wife of John Taylor, in 1830. They became best friends and close confidants, although it is unclear when or if their relationship became sexual in a physical sense. Although it is difficult today to imagine that two heterosexuals in love could avoid physical intimacy for over twenty years, their correspondence suggests they did not. And why would they lie to themselves? Mill in his autobiography suggests it did not until after their marriage in 1851 (John Taylor died in 1849). But by this time, Harriet was quite ill. She had 'consumption' (it is now believed that this is tuberculosis) and would die in Avignon, France in 1858 (two months after Mill retires). Mill will later die of the same cause in Avignon on 7 May 1873. Harriet's daughter, Helen, replaced her as Mill's companion, and Mill refers to her as 'his daughter' in his autobiography. There is no hint of any impropriety in this relationship. Helen would posthumously publish the *Autobiography* and 'Chapters on Socialism.'

However we are to interpret Mill and Harriet's relationship, it was scandalous in Victorian terms. Married women did not have 'relationships,' whatever this consists of, with men other than their husbands. This led to a further deterioration of the relationship between Mill and his family. Mill's mother is not mentioned once in his autobiography.

A point of contention is how influential Harriet was on Mill's written work. Mill's praise of her is unqualified in some places, referring to her in the *Autobiography* as the joint author of much of his work, and having a superior intellect to his own.

The dedication to *On Liberty* reads:

> To the beloved and deplored memory of her who was the inspirer, and part author, of all that's best in my writings – the friend and wife whose exalted sense of truth and right was my strongest incitement and whose approbation was my chief reward – I dedicate this volume. Like all that I have written for many years, it belongs as much to her as to me; but the work as it stands has had, in a very insufficient degree, the inestimable advantage of her revision, some of the most important portions having been reserved for a more careful reexamination, which they are now never destined to receive. Were I but capable of interpreting to the world one half the great thoughts and noble feelings which are buried in her grave, I should be the medium of a greater benefit to it, than is ever likely to arise from anything that I can write, unprompted and unassisted by her all but unrivaled wisdom.[16]

Other contemporaries, such as Bain, found her to be intellectually quite ordinary. Like the nature of their sexual relationship, their intellectual relationship is in dispute as well.

vi. THE ANCIENT GREEKS

The influence of the Greeks and Greek philosophy on John Stuart Mill's education has been noted by many commentators (most importantly, Mill himself in his autobiography as discussed earlier). But it is strikingly rare to see commentators try to explain ambiguities in Mill's thought with reference to problems or attempted resolutions of problems that one can find in ancient philosophy. This is an interesting omission, particularly in analysis of Mill's *Utilitarianism*, a work that is not only peppered with references to the Greeks but also at one point uses an Epicurean response to answer charges brought against utilitarianism. In fact, the first paragraph of this work contains a reference to Plato's *Protagoras*, which I will discuss later. Now the inclusion of this reference is clearly not surprising; Plato has Socrates discuss weighing and measuring goods in a manner that can easily be interpreted as proto-utilitarian (I will discuss this later). This could simply be a literary device for giving utilitarianism as an ethical theory a long and cherished past. But there are other places that Mill could have grounded himself, and what must be noted is Mill's decision to use Plato and in particular the *Protagoras*. I believe there is a reading of Mill that will not find this inclusion parenthetical. My purpose in the next few paragraphs will be to examine why this work, and what Mill had to say about it, could be important for the further explication of Mill's thought.

vii. THE DIALOGUES OF PLATO

Mill wrote what has been called 'commentary/translations' on nine of the dialogues of Plato, five of which were published during his lifetime.[17] I am calling these 'commentary/translations' to give the reader here a flavor of what is going on. At times Mill is satisfied to merely translate; at other times he briefly summarizes long passages. His comments, when he makes them, are not really criticisms but rather attempts to help his audience to grasp what is at stake in the dialogues. When one is reading these commentary/translations it becomes quite apparent that for the most part Mill wishes his audience to be introduced to Plato first hand (or at least to what Mill takes to be an unbiased reading). The first of these to be published was on the *Protagoras*. His purpose in writing these commentary/translations is clearly spelled out:

> Considering the almost boundless reputation of the writings of Plato, not only among scholars, but (upon their authority) among nearly all who have any tincture of letters, it is a remarkable fact, that of the great writers of antiquity, there is scarcely one who, in this country at least, is not merely so little understood but so little read.[18]

Thus, Mill's purpose is clear enough; he wishes to bring Plato to a wider audience. His choice of the *Protagoras* is, however, interesting and his way of setting it up even more so. The *Protagoras*, like many of the early dialogues of Plato, concerns itself with a central question: in this case 'can virtue be taught?'. But it differs from the early dialogues in at least two important respects. The first is that while the elder Protagoras is ultimately to be vanquished by the younger

Socrates, he is in many ways the bearer of common sense. As Mill puts it 'what he utters is by no means either absurd or immoral, but on the contrary, sound and useful good sense.'[19] The second is that by the time the dialogue ends they seem to have switched positions (initially Protagoras seemed to be claiming that virtue could be taught and Socrates was skeptical, by the end Socrates finds this thesis more plausible than he initially did and Protagoras is beginning to have doubts); but not conclusively so and in a manner that is not terribly convincing. The dialogue ends with Socrates noting that having disagreed on the intermediate question, 'does virtue consist of knowledge?', it seems that they may have switched sides on the central question. Socrates, having successfully argued for the 'unity of the virtues,' must find that virtue consists of knowledge and knowledge, at least plausibly, is something that can be taught. But is the kind of knowledge that virtue consists in something that can be taught? This has yet to be demonstrated. Thus, it does not appear that Plato has answered the central question of the dialogue but rather has demonstrated how the debate could go. For Mill, this is the central importance of the work:

> There is no work of Plato which more obviously appears to have been intended rather as an exercise in the art of investigating truth, than to inculcate any particular set of philosophical opinions. Many ingenious and profound thoughts are, indeed, thrown out in the course of the discussion. But even if we had to form our judgement of this dialogue without the light thrown upon it by the other works of Plato, we should be compelled to draw up one of two conclusions; either the author had not yet made up his opinions on the topics treated in the dialogue, or that he did not think this a proper place for unfolding them.[20]

The question arises, then, in light of the above passage and Mill's unequivocal stance on the importance of Plato, why this is the dialogue that Mill wishes his audience to begin with. I think the key will be found in recognizing the fundamental purpose of investigating truth even if one does not expect to actually find it. Mill does not seem to fault Plato in the least for either not having made up his mind or not being ready to divulge his opinion to his audience. Part of the reason for this, I will argue later, is that this is a common Millian rhetorical device; Plato has an answer but he wishes us to struggle with the puzzle a little longer. The power of this dialogue rests not in its ability to give the reader some received 'truth' but rather in its power to develop reasoning skills. Whatever 'truth' there is to be had can be found in the dialectical process that Socrates and his opponent(s) engage in. The reason why Mill, I think quite rightly, values this dialogue so highly is that it highlights the importance of the dialectical process itself. Socrates and Protagoras do not answer the question they set out to answer; but they do engage each other in a way that is illuminating to the audience. The victor here is not so much Socrates, but rather, the Socratic method. Plato allows Socrates and the dialectical method a chance to show why this method is more likely to produce knowledge than the didactic method of Protagoras and the Sophists. As Mill puts it:

> If it be possible, therefore to assign any specific and decided purpose to this dialogue, it would appear to be intended not to hold up the Sophists either to ridicule or obloquy, but to show that it was possible to go much beyond the point which they had attained in moral and political philosophy; that, on the whole they left the science of mind and virtue in an extremely unsatisfactory state; that they could not stand the test of the rigorous dialectics which Socrates carried into these inquiries; and that the truth could only be ascertained by that more accurate mode of sifting opinions, which the dialectic method . . . furnishes, but which speech making, and the mere delivery of doctrines from master to student (the practice of the Sophists) absolutely preclude.[21]

The importance of this for understanding Mill's own work is, I think, enormous. Mill does not wish to simply hand us the answers to important questions (I am not even sure he would think there are any absolute answers, but more on this later). He wants us to see the reasoning that led to the answer. The central importance of the *Protagoras*, then, is that it marks an important moment in the progress of philosophical method. Often discussions of the importance of the Platonic dialogues is limited to their content; Mill wishes to stress that this overemphasis on the content of the dialogues comes at the expense of neglecting the philosophical method that Plato employs. The old ways of the Sophists must be replaced by those of Plato and his heirs if progress is to take place (but more on the importance of progress in this discussion later).

viii. THE LOGIC OF ARISTOTLE

Mill elaborates on these issues in his discussion of Grote's *Aristotle*. He remarks favorably upon Grote's decision to 'copiously' analyze a treatise of Aristotle's, the *Topica* (included in the *Organon*), since it is of 'great importance to a correct understanding of the Greek mind.' According to Mill, this treatise on 'Dialectic Reasoning,' 'the art of arguing for victory, not for truth,' is initially difficult to reconcile with the other writings of Aristotle because of Aristotle's usual 'indefatigable ardor in the pursuit of truth.'[22] Mill first points out the importance of physical and mental contests for ancient Greek societies, through which it was possible to acquire honor for oneself and one's city. Thus, it would be only natural that Dialectics, defined by Mill as the 'regulated discussion by question and answer,' would itself become a popular 'game.'[23] This dialectical game would function in much the same way that basketball functions on the playgrounds of our society today. The way this game works one starts with a thesis, usually on some important or interesting topic, a probable opinion either held by most people or by some respected authority, which one individual agrees to defend against a group of opponents. The opponents are allowed to ask questions that can be explicitly answered 'yes' or 'no' and if the respondent can be forced into admissions that are either inconsistent with each other or with the thesis, then the opponents have won the contest. Otherwise, the proponent is the victor. Thus the participants in this game are given the opportunity to engage themselves in a regulated and disciplined activity; one designed to determine whether a proponent can maintain a thesis without falling into inconsistency or contradiction.

Mill thinks that Aristotle is completely justified in giving instruction for this kind of contest, for Aristotle rightly thinks that these contests are 'of great utility in reference to the pursuit of truth.'[24] Mill now cites Grote as offering three points in support of these contests. First, engaging in these debates is a stimulating exercise for those who participate. Secondly, by bringing oneself into contact with the opinions of others it allows one to 'note and remember the opinions of the multitude.'[25] This knowledge is important since if we wish to modify the behavior of others it will be important to be able to converse with them in terms of opinions that they are already familiar with. Mill finds this aspect of Aristotle's philosophy important because it distinguishes Aristotle from those who held that the philosopher ought 'to keep aloof from the multitude and withdraw from the duty of advising them for their own good by arguments drawn from their own opinions.'[26] Thirdly, and most importantly, this dialectic debate has a profound, if indirect, influence on the methodology of both science and philosophy and for evaluating whatever truths that these disciplines may uncover. Engaging in this dialectic debate habituates us to the examination of a question from different and often opposing points of view. By examining the difficulties associated with any given point of view, by noting the problems associated with taking either side of a given thesis, we are then better prepared for 'detecting and discriminating truth and falsehood.'[27] Mill, in extremely unequivocal praise of Aristotle, offers us an important insight into how he thinks one can search for the truth.

> Of this benefit from dialectic exercise, Aristotle's practice affords a remarkable verification: for he very frequently commences his investigation of a difficult question by a detailed enumeration and statement of the aporia, the difficulties or puzzles, which affect it; and there is no way in which his method of studying a subject sets a more beneficial example. In this respect he was greatly in advance not only of his own time, but of ours. His general advice for exercise and practice in Dialectic is admirably adapted to the training of one's own mind for the pursuit of truth. You ought to test every thesis by first assuming it to be true, then assuming it to be false, and following the consequences out on both sides.[28]

Now, despite his praise of Aristotle given here, Mill recognizes that the dialectic contests of the Greeks were far from an infallible method of securing truth. He also acknowledges that there may be better methods available; it could be that other means would allow one to get at the truth more easily. But the fact remains that 'no such means has been provided' and the valuable training of the mind provided by this method has not been replaced with some other but has rather been allowed to disappear. In fact, Mill finds this a major failure of the education offered the young of his own time. He thinks that in principle there can be no justification for the abandonment of 'a practice so useful for the pursuit of truth,' particularly when 'the attainment of truth is the sole object.' He believes that the dialectic method of the Greeks could be usefully employed in all disciplines and branches of higher education and this would clearly be done if teachers thought it was 'part of their business to form thinkers' rather than, as Mill suggests Locke puts it, ' "principling" their pupils . . . with ready made knowledge.'[29]

Before we leave Mill's discussion of Grote's *Aristotle*, there is one more issue I would like to take up. The careful reader at this point may well be asking why have I initially placed my insistence on the importance of Plato and the Greeks to Mill rather than to the importance of Aristotle? The point is that Mill has a fundamental disagreement with Aristotle and the other Greek philosophers over an issue that Mill thinks Plato gets right. Thus, while the Greek methodology is common to all, there is an important reason for Mill to ultimately wish to align the dialectic method he intends to use in his political philosophy more closely with Plato's rather than with Aristotle's (later I will argue that there are other aspects of Aristotle that Mill will definitely wish to use). Mill is a firm believer in progress. He, of course, lived at a time when one could easily believe that advances in technology and freedom will allow for better and better societies to develop. He has the progressives' firm belief in the possibility of change for the better. Aristotle, of course, lived during the tail end of Athenian democracy. He would have no reason to have any other than the conservatives' desire to maintain the good that presently exists. Plato and Mill may have different visions of how to improve society but they both believe in the possibility of meaningful change. On Mill's account, Aristotle and the other Greek philosophers of this era lack this vision. Speaking of Aristotle's *Politics* Mill writes:

> *The Politics*, in lieu of the adventurous anticipations of genius which we find in *The Republic* of Plato, present us with the mode of thinking of a Liberal Conservative, or rather, of a moderately aristocratical politician at Athens. In the main, it is a philosophic consecration of existing facts (witness its strange defence of slavery), choosing by preference among those facts such as tend towards stability, rather than towards improvement. It should be remembered that, unless so far as Plato may be considered an exception, none of the ancient politicians or philosophers believed in progress; their highest hopes were limited to guarding society against its natural tendency to degeneration.[30]

Thus the importance of Plato and in particular Plato's *Protagoras* is twofold. We are introduced to a dialectical method of great importance that is an improvement on what was previously available. Thus we have both the dialectical method and the notion of progress being introduced. Mill does not wish us to view Socrates as merely a clever debater armed with a weapon that Protagoras has no defense against. Socrates actually is a seeker of truth. He wishes to use his method to make things more intelligible to all; Socrates is not merely trying to win arguments. One perhaps may learn the Greek dialectical method as one would learn to play basketball. One studies the moves of the great players, practices these moves and develops one's own and then finally employs them in contests to sharpen one's skills. For Mill, however, it will be important to distinguish between how one develops a talent and the ultimate purpose of attaining a talent. Ultimately the purpose of learning the dialectical method will be to increase and improve the stock of available human wisdom. It will allow us access to whatever truth we can hope to attain; for Mill truth will be the fuel that feeds progress. If the dialectical method is used properly, then it will ultimately lead to progress, which is all that Mill thinks one could really hope for.

Thus, it is the Greeks as well as the British Empiricists who are the foundations of the falliblism, as described in the last chapter by Skorupski, that forms the basis for Mill's philosophy.

ix. PLATO AND UTILITARIANISM

Finally, if one is so inclined, one can trace the history of utilitarianism back to Plato. In fact, the influential Plato scholar, C.D.C. Reeve, in his *Philosopher-Kings: The Argument of Plato's Republic* calls Plato a 'character-utilitarian.'[31] Although Reeves is the only author I am aware of who makes this point explicitly, there are passages in the *Republic* and other dialogues that support this view. So, for example, in Book IV of the *Republic* Socrates is discussing his ideal community with Adeimantus. After Socrates puts limits on the freedom of the Philosopher Kings who will rule this ideal community, Adeimantus wonders if this will make the Philosopher Kings unhappy. Socrates replies:

> We'll reply that although it wouldn't surprise us in the slightest if in fact there were no people happier than those men, all the same we're not constructing our community with the intention of making one group within it especially happy, but to maximize the happiness of the community as a whole . . . What we are doing at the moment, we think, is forming a community as a whole, without having off a few of its members and making them the happy ones . . .[32]

Similarly, in a discussion with Protagoras in the *Protagoras* Socrates tells us the following:

> For if anyone says, Yes, Socrates, but the pleasure of the moment differs widely from future pleasure and pain, to that I should reply: And do they differ in anything but pleasure and pain? There is nothing else. And do you, like a skillful weigher, put in the balance the pleasures and the pains, and their nearness and distance, and then say which outweighs the other? If you measure pleasures against pleasures you should take the more and greater; or if you weigh pains against pains, you should take the fewer and less . . .[33]

Although it is a point of contention among Plato scholars to what extent the views indicated above are Plato's, or Socrates's or some mixture of the two, the point does not concern us. The point that we are interested in is that we can trace two proto-utilitarian claims back to Plato. First, in the *Republic* it is suggested that an ideal society will maximize utility, and, secondly, in the *Protagoras* it is suggested that utility can be cashed out in terms of weighing and balancing pleasures and pains. Similarly, there have been attempts to trace utilitarianism to Hume and others who can be interpreted as consequentialist moral philosophers.

But I think these approaches are misguided. Utilitarianism as presented to us in its eighteenth and nineteenth century forms offers more to its supporters than its consequentialism and egalitarianism. The utilitarian radicals of this era owe as much to Locke's empiricism, political liberalism, and faith in democracy. Plato was neither an empiricist nor a liberal, and Plato's republic is not a democracy. It is to this political liberalism that I know turn my attention.

CHAPTER 3

LIBERALISM AND *ON LIBERTY*

i. CLASSICAL ECONOMICS AND ADAM SMITH

The first major theorist in classical economics, or political economy, as it was then called, was Adam Smith (1723–1790). Other major thinkers that are commonly included in this group include Thomas Malthus (1766–1834), Jean-Baptiste Say (1767–1834), David Ricardo (1772–1823), Frederic Bastiat (1801–1850).

Smith's major economic work was *An Inquiry into the Nature and Causes of the Wealth of Nations* (1776). Although Smith is primarily known as an economist today, he was hired in 1751 to teach logic at Glasgow university, and spent an additional fourteen years there as the Chair of Moral Philosophy. It was commonly held in the twentieth century, and perhaps still commonly held by many today, that the nineteenth century classical economists all held an extreme form of laissez faire economics. It is suggested that they believed that all governmental interference with the free market was suspect, since the market was best governed by market forces beyond our powers of understanding and control. This view that markets should always be left to their own devices is nowadays termed 'libertarianism.' Libertarians often believe that there should be little or no regulation of social aspects of human life as well; libertarians typically reject laws against, say, drug use or prostitution. These libertarians often write as if all the classical liberals and classical economists clearly supported the strongest form of laissez faire economics. In my opinion, among the classical economists listed above, only Bastiat was an unqualified libertarian. Bastiat's work is often cited favorably by a major libertarian economic school known as Austrian Economics. In fact, Bastiat's 'broken widow fallacy' and Smith's 'invisible hand' are often used to explain laissez faire thought. In this section I will concentrate on Smith. Adam Smith's 'invisible hand' is purportedly the paradigm and exemplar of the laissez faire view. The idea is rather than allow the clumsy fist of governmental authority to make economic policy decisions, the invisible hand of the market would lead to the best overall results. As the invisible hand is usually presented, the idea is that when large numbers of independent people make decisions in the marketplace, these individual decisions work as an invisible hand guiding resources to their most efficient use. An individual regulator or regulating body could never understand or approximate the wisdom that is produced by large numbers of consumers and entrepreneurs acting on their individual choices. When presented with this libertarian view, Thomas Carlyle referred to economics as 'the dismal science,' a phrase that critics of economic theory still use today.

However recent critics have noted that this view is minimally a gross simplification of even Smith's actual views, and probably an out and out distortion. Jonathan Schefler has argued in his 'Today's Most Mischievous Misquotation' that Smith's invisible hand is 'one of the most distorted passages in economics literature.'[1] As proof Schefler cites the following passage from what he calls 'the leading college text on the subject since the 1950s,' Samuelson's *Economics*. Samuelson cites a crucial passage from Adam Smith's *Wealth of Nations* in the following misleading fashion:

> Every individual endeavors to employ his capital so that its produce may be of greatest value. He generally neither intends to promote the public interest, nor knows how much he is promoting it. *He intends only his own security, only his own gain. And he is in this led by an invisible hand to promote an end which was no part of his own intention.* By pursuing his own interest he frequently promotes that of society more effectually that when he really intends to promote it. [italics added by Schefler][2]

However, Samuelson and Nordhaus have 'concocted' a 'typical variant' of the received reading of *The Wealth of Nations*. The underlined portion of the above quote has been 'reworked' by 'chopping and splicing without using ellipses.'[3] Smith actually wrote:

> By preferring the support of domestic to foreign industry, he intends only his own security; and by directing that industry in such a manner as its produce may be of the greatest value, he intends only his own gain, and he is in this, as in many other cases, led by an invisible hand to promote an end which was no part of his intention.[4]

Thus, far from being a libertarian rallying cry, the 'invisible hand' serves the limited purpose of promoting overall societal good by leading investors to domestic rather than foreign investment. Of course, someone advocating this theory today would be required to engage in some fancy footwork; after all, in today's world it is very common for investors to 'support foreign industry.' Schefler goes on to note that a twentieth-century perspective often obscures Smith's major agenda; he was a staunch opponent of British mercantilism, a system of monopolies where the third world was divided into various parcels and various companies were given an exclusive contract to trade certain goods with each. This was consistent with the mercantilist's view that a nation's prosperity was best determined by the wealth it held in gold and other scarce resources that were used in monetary exchange. To accomplish this goal, trade with our nations should serve the purpose of creating a net balance of exports over imports. Policies concerning subsidies and taxes should be employed to further this goal as well. Two of Smith's goals in the *Wealth of Nations* were to argue against this conception of 'wealth,' and that the interests of a 'nation' were not the same as that of nation's aristocracy. Obviously, one can oppose mercantilism without supporting laissez faire economics.

At other places in the *Wealth of Nations* Smith comes closer to endorsing the traditional interpretation of the invisible hand. But often the view is put forward in a manner that makes the concept implausible. But even in the closest endorsement for the view usually associated with the invisible hand that I am aware of, there is no clear rejection of any interference on the part of the government in all cases. Smith writes:

> Every individual is continually exerting himself to find out the most advantageous employment for whatever capital he can command. It is his own advantage, indeed, and not that of the society, which he has in view. But the study of his own advantage

> naturally, or rather necessarily, leads him to prefer that employment which is most advantageous to the society.[5]

If this claim were true, then traditional reading of the invisible might follow. But does anyone actually believe that every time anyone employs their capital the greatest good for society is produced? Every time a street dealer sells crack to an addict, this is the most efficient use of their time and capital, not just for them, but for society as a whole? As a matter of necessity? As we shall see later in this work, the relationship between human freedom and the common good is quite complex; as we shall see later, a central question for Mill is how to reconcile individual liberty with the common good. But as baldly stated as Smith offers it to us here, it seems beyond defense.

The issue is further clouded when one compares Smith's views in *The Wealth of Nations* with his earlier *The Theory of Moral Sentiments*. As noted earlier, Smith was a professor of moral philosophy, and his earlier work emphasizes the universality and primacy of sympathy as a source of human morality. The difficulty of reconciling Smith's emphasis on sympathy in *Moral Sentiments* with the emphasis on self-interest in *Wealth of Nations* even has a name in the Smith secondary literature; it is called 'the Adam Smith Problem.'[6] Although I am not interested in solving this issue, it only takes a brief perusal of the secondary literature to recognize it is real. Those who wish to read Smith as an unabashed advocate of free market economics often 'solve' this problem by ignoring it. However, even if one ignores this problem, Smith is hardly a libertarian champion. Read alone, Smith's *Wealth of Nations* offers qualified support, for example, of public education.[7]

Smith and the *Wealth of Nations* also is hardly a ringing endorsement for the character of capitalists. In fact, he distrusted their motives, and thought they had little commitment to the moral life. Smith writes:

> People of the same trade seldom meet together, even for merriment and diversion, but the conversation ends in a conspiracy against the public, or in some contrivance to raise prices. It is impossible indeed to prevent such meetings, by any law which either could be executed, or would be consistent with liberty and justice. But though the law cannot hinder people of the same

> trade from sometimes assembling together, it ought to do nothing to facilitate such assemblies; much less to render them necessary.[8]

Thus, the business community, if given the opportunity, would be happy to conspire against the public. But as a matter of efficiency, there is little to be done. From the perspective of a non-consequentialist morality, that is, one that puts moral principles above results, Smith's argument here would be morally unsound. Smith must be arguing that the ends do justify the means in this case. In this case, it would be impossible to hinder such meetings without unintended consequences in other areas. Once again, Smith's 'factual claim' here is troubling. Why is it that such regulations cannot be implemented to prevent conspiracies against the public? But most importantly, laissez faire is not being endorsed as a moral principle, but rather as a general rule that in many cases leads to good results.

> It is not from the benevolence of the butcher, the brewer, or the baker, that we expect our dinner, but from their regard to their own interest. We address ourselves, not to their humanity but to their self-love, and never talk to them of our own necessities but of their advantages.[9]

Once again, the advocate of laissez faire points out that individual self-interest can lead to the betterment of society. But let us not put the cart in front of the horse. The free market and individual self interest when it works well is remarkably efficient and can lead to promoting the common good. But what to do when it does not? Whenever Smith seems to be promoting individual self interest or the free market, he seems to do so for consequentialist reasons, not non-consequentialist moral principles.

So if the point of the *Wealth of Nations* is not a non-consequentialist moral defense of laissez faire capitalism, or an endorsement for the moral sensibilities of capitalists, what is it that Smith wishes to accomplish? It seems to be to describe situations where the proper use of economic principles can lead to greater wealth for the community at large.

ii. SMITH AND THE DIVISION OF LABOR

One example that Smith uses in the *Wealth of Nations* to make this point concerns the advantages in many situations of the division of labor. I do not wish to suggest that the division of labor was Smith's only contribution to economics, but his contribution here is clear and often noted. When different individuals hold different occupations, as is often offered in industrial economies, the division of labor can be an important contributor to the wealth of the people. Smith writes:

> To take an example, therefore, from a very trifling manufacture; but one in which the division of labour has been very often taken notice of, the trade of the pin-maker; a workman not educated to this business (which the division of labour has rendered a distinct trade), nor acquainted with the use of the machinery employed in it (to the invention of which the same division of labour has probably given occasion), could scarce, perhaps, with his utmost industry, make one pin in a day, and certainly could not make twenty.[10]

Thus, if one asked an untrained individual to make a simple object like a pin, that individual would find it an amazingly difficult task. As a by-product of this, without the division of labor, pins would be prohibitively expensive. But since one can divide the job of makings pins into several parts, and train a different person to do the part that they know how to do, it is possible to make pins more efficiently. Smith continues:

> But in the way in which this business is now carried on, not only the whole work is a peculiar trade, but it is divided into a number of branches, of which the greater part are likewise peculiar trades. One man draws out the wire, another straights it, a third cuts it, a fourth points it, a fifth grinds it at the top for receiving, the head; to make the head requires two or three distinct operations; to put it on is a peculiar business, to whiten the pins is another; it is even a trade by itself to put them into the paper; and the important business of making a pin is, in this manner, divided into about eighteen distinct operations, which, in some manufactories, are all performed by distinct hands, though in others the same man will sometimes perform two or three of them.

> I have seen a small manufactory of this kind where ten men only were employed, and where some of them consequently performed two or three distinct operations. But though they were very poor, and therefore but indifferently accommodated with the necessary machinery, they could, when they exerted themselves, make among them about twelve pounds of pins in a day. There are in a pound upwards of four thousand pins of a middling size. Those ten persons, therefore, could make among them upwards of forty-eight thousand pins in a day.[11]

Through a process of dividing the labor into separate jobs, the pin factory workers can increase their individual productivity. Whereas one person working alone can produce few if any pins, ten people acting in concert can produce a large number of pins. Thus, the division of labor accomplishes two important goals. One, it allows each worker to vastly increase his or her own productivity. As individuals they are not productive, but as a group they are. Two, it allows pins to be produced so efficiently, that pins can be made available to the public at a reasonable price. In this case, the workers, the factory owner, and the general public should all benefit from an efficient use of the division of labor. Smith concludes:

> Each person, therefore, making a tenth part of forty-eight thousand pins, might be considered as making four thousand eight hundred pins in a day. But if they had all wrought separately and independently, and without any of them having been educated to this peculiar business, they certainly could not each of them have made twenty, perhaps not one pin in a day; that is, certainly, not the two hundred and fortieth, perhaps not the four thousand eight hundredth part of what they are at present capable of performing, in consequence of a proper division and combination of their different operations.[12]

It is in this kind of passage that Smith is at his best. There is no suggestion that making pins is the best use of the time and resources of the factory owner and the laborers. There is no suggestion that the employment of resources in this case necessarily produces the best overall societal outcome. Rather, the claim is more modest; if you are going to make pins, the division of labor as described above, seems the most efficient way to go. The title of Smith's economics work really tells the story central to many of the classical economists. The classical economists were interested in increasing the wealth of the people, not the aristocracy, and were inquiring into the causes that made it possible.

iii. *ON LIBERTY* AND THE *AUTOBIOGRAPHY*

In his autobiography Mill argues for the importance of his wife's influence on his work overall, and the particular influence that she had on *On Liberty*. He describes *On Liberty* as being 'directly and literally our joint production . . . for there was not a sentence of it that was not several times gone through by us together.' Mill credits this joint production as far surpassing 'anything which has proceeded from me either before or since.' As usual in these cases where Mill is giving Harriet such extreme praise, one can speculate as to the degree of hyperbole. But it is clear that with or without Harriet's help, Mill considered the final product his finest work. He tells us that there were times in his 'mental progress' where he could have 'fallen into a tendency towards over-government, both social and political; as there was also a moment when, by reaction from a contrary excess, I might have become a less thorough radical and democrat than I am.'[13] As noted earlier, there will always be some tension in being both a liberal and a utilitarian, and to some degree one judges the importance of Mill's ethical and political philosophy by how well he manages to resolve this tension. One key trap that a liberal must avoid falling into is to be too accepting of alternate views, and thus losing sight of essential truths. Mill credits Harriet with helping him in this regard.

> My great readiness and eagerness to learn from everybody, and to make room in my opinions for every new acquisition by adjusting the old and the new to one another, might, but for her steadying influence, have seduced me into modifying my early opinions too much. She was in nothing more valuable to my mental development than by her just measure of the relative importance of different considerations, which often protected me from allowing to truths I had only recently learnt to see, a more important place in my thoughts than was properly their due.[14]

However one resolves the 'Harriet Question' it is clear that she served Mill well as a 'sounding board,' where he could bounce new ideas around and see how they sounded. Once again, if Mill is to be believed, however one interprets Harriet's role, this collaboration hits its zenith in *On Liberty*, and Mill ultimately describes it as his most successful project.

> The 'Liberty' is likely to survive longer than anything else that I have written (with the possible exception of the 'Logic'), because the conjunction of her mind with mine has rendered it a kind of philosophic text-book of a single truth, which the changes progressively taking place in modern society tend to bring out into ever stronger relief: the importance, to man and society of a large variety in types of character, and of giving full freedom to human nature to expand itself in innumerable and conflicting directions.[15]

Thus Mill enunciates the central ideas of this work, namely, the importance of human freedom, the importance of character development, and the close interaction between the two. If human beings are to be free in any meaningful sense of the word, they must be free to develop their own characters. Otherwise, we find ourselves in a situation where we can suffer under the tyranny of the majority. It is not enough that we have options; we must have options that are our own.

> Nothing can better show how deep are the foundations of this truth, than the great impression made by the exposition of it at a time which, to superficial observation, did not seem to stand much in need of such a lesson. The fears we expressed, lest the inevitable growth of social equality and of the government of public opinion, should impose on mankind an oppressive yoke of uniformity in opinion and practice, might easily have appeared chimerical to those who looked more at present facts than at tendencies; for the gradual revolution that is taking place in society and institutions has, thus far, been decidedly favourable to the development of new opinions, and has procured for them a much more unprejudiced hearing than they previously met with.[16]

To the superficial observer, this truth does not seem of great importance in Mill's time, as there seems to be a gradual acceptance of cultural diversity. But this is illusiory. It is only because there are times when cultures find themselves open to ideas. During these times there is no sense of danger.

> But this is a feature belonging to periods of transition, when old notions and feelings have been unsettled, and no new doctrines have yet succeeded to their ascendancy. At such times people of any mental activity, having given up many of their old beliefs, and not feeling quite sure that those they still retain can stand unmodified, listen eagerly to new opinions.[17]

When the status quo is not working, when institutions are failing, the people are open to change. But institutions eventually resolve their difficulties, and immediate problems are resolved, and when societies settle down and solve their transitional problems, the danger is still lurking.

> But this state of things is necessarily transitory: some particular body of doctrine in time rallies the majority round it, organizes social institutions and modes of action conformably to itself, education impresses this new creed upon the new generations without the mental processes that have led to it, and by degrees it acquires the very same power of compression, so long exercised by the creeds of which it had taken the place. Whether this noxious power will be exercised, depends on whether mankind have by that time become aware that it cannot be exercised without stunting and dwarfing human nature. It is then that the teachings of the 'Liberty' will have their greatest value. And it is to be feared that they will retain that value a long time.[18]

Thus, openness to the new and different will be accepted when times cry out for change. But what will happen when the status quo seems fine? Mill's answer is that in these times, the truths contained in *On Liberty* will be essential.

Thus, freedom must be defended even when its usefulness is not readily apparent. But what freedoms are to be defended. In chapter V of *On Liberty* Mill clarifies the fact that he is not endorsing libertarian economic freedom. He writes:

> Again, trade is a social act. Whoever undertakes to sell any description of goods to the public, does what affects the interest of other persons, and of society in general; and thus his conduct, in principle, comes within the jurisdiction of society: accordingly, it was once held to be the duty of governments, in all cases which were considered of importance, to fix prices, and regulate the processes of manufacture.[19]

Thus, Mill finds the regulation of economic matters fair game for the state. But does that mean that he thinks the state should interfere willy-nilly? No, as a classical economist Mill thinks that laissez faire economics should be the rule, and regulation should be minimal. But the reasons for laissez faire economics are practical and not the essential principle that underlies *On Liberty*.

> But it is now recognised, though not till after a long struggle, that both the cheapness and the good quality of commodities are most effectually provided for by leaving the producers and sellers perfectly free, under the sole check of equal freedom to the buyers for supplying themselves elsewhere. This is the so-called doctrine of Free Trade, which rests on grounds different from, though equally solid with, the principle of individual liberty asserted in this Essay.[20]

If Mill is not defending libertarian economic freedom in *On Liberty*, what exactly is he defending? In a previous chapter I mentioned the importance of character formation for Mill. For Mill, as I will elaborate in what follows, character development is a 'paramount end' which in some cases can even override in the short run the principle of utility. A thesis central to this work is that the freedoms Mill is advocating in *On Liberty* are those that he finds essential to individual moral growth and character formation. The aphorism 'you cannot legislate morality' is often interpreted vacuously; as if punitive laws, say, against drug use or prostitution simply will not work. Although behaviorists have claimed that positive and negative reinforcement are more efficient than punishment, clearly a sufficient punishment will have some deterrent effect. In one important sense much of all we legislate is morality. We have laws against murder precisely because we believe that some forms of homicide are unjustified and therefore wrong. But in another sense, this expression is true. Passing legislation may deter behavior, but it may not make people want to be moral. Similarly, Mill will recognize that laws that restrict fundamental freedoms are contrary to public policy goals that require that citizens desire to be moral. Laws that stifle individual freedom may change behavior, but they do so at a cost on individual moral growth and character development. The freedoms Mill is advocating in *On Liberty* are those freedoms that allow individuals to flourish, to find their own way, to be the best person they can possibly be. In the first chapter of *On Liberty* Mill writes:

> But there is a sphere of action in which society, as distinguished from the individual, has, if any, only an indirect interest; comprehending all that portion of a person's life and conduct which affects only himself, or if it also affects others, only with their free, voluntary, and undeceived consent and participation. When I say only himself, I mean directly, and in the first instance: for whatever affects himself, may affect others through himself; and the objection which may be grounded on this contingency, will receive consideration in the sequel. This, then, is the appropriate region of human liberty. It comprises, first, the inward domain of consciousness; demanding liberty of conscience, in the most comprehensive sense; liberty of thought and feeling; absolute freedom of opinion and sentiment on all subjects, practical or speculative, scientific, moral, or theological. The liberty of expressing and publishing opinions may seem to fall under a different principle, since it belongs to that part of the conduct of an individual which concerns other people; but, being almost of as much importance as the liberty of thought itself, and resting in great part on the same reasons, is practically inseparable from it. Secondly, the principle requires liberty of tastes and pursuits; of framing the plan of our life to suit our own character; of doing as we like, subject to such consequences as may follow: without impediment from our fellow-creatures, so long as what we do does not harm them, even though they should think our conduct foolish, perverse, or wrong. Thirdly, from this liberty of each individual, follows the liberty, within the same limits, of combination among individuals; freedom to unite, for any purpose not involving harm to others: the persons combining being supposed to be of full age, and not forced or deceived.[21]

The principle freedoms that Mill is advocating are those of thought, expression, and association. According to Mill, if one is to be the master of one's own destiny, it is critical to have these freedoms, and in his scheme the latter two are clearly derivative from the first. Freedom of thought would be of little value if one was not free to test one's ideas in the intellectual marketplace. To develop one's thought in full it is necessary to subject one's ideas to the scrutiny of others. In order to do this you must be free to express yourself to others and be free to associate with others that find your questions to be critical ones.

> No society in which these liberties are not, on the whole, respected, is free, whatever may be its form of government; and none is completely free in which they do not exist absolute and unqualified. The only freedom which deserves the name, is that of pursuing our own good in our own way, so long as we do not attempt to deprive others of theirs, or impede their efforts to obtain it. Each is the proper guardian of his own health, whether bodily, or mental or spiritual. Mankind are greater gainers by suffering each other to live as seems good to themselves, than by compelling each to live as seems good to the rest.[22]

The noted exception to this is when our conduct is 'harmful' to others. This notion of harm is central to Mill's social and political philosophy, and *On Liberty* is the work where he explicates it most carefully. It is to this that I now turn my attention.

iv. THE HARM PRINCIPLE

Many readers of Mill, particularly those in the legal community, find *On Liberty* to be advocating what has been come to be known as 'the Harm Principle' (sometimes commentators use the alternate 'Harm-to-Others Principle'). Supporters for this view generally stress the following passage.

> The object of this Essay is to assert one very simple principle, as entitled to govern absolutely the dealings of society with the individual in the way of compulsion and control, whether the means used be physical force in the form of legal penalties, or the moral coercion of public opinion. That principle is, that the sole

> end for which mankind are warranted, individually or collectively, in interfering with the liberty of action of any of their number, is self-protection. That the only purpose for which power can be rightfully exercised over any member of a civilized community, against his will, is to prevent harm to others. His own good, either physical or moral, is not a sufficient warrant. He cannot rightfully be compelled to do or forbear because it will be better for him to do so, because it will make him happier, because, in the opinions of others, to do so would be wise, or even right. These are good reasons for remonstrating with him, or reasoning with him, or persuading him, or entreating him, but not for compelling him, or visiting him with any evil in case he do otherwise. To justify that, the conduct from which it is desired to deter him, must be calculated to produce evil to some one else. The only part of the conduct of any one, for which he is amenable to society, is that which concerns others. In the part which merely concerns himself, his independence is, of right, absolute. Over himself, over his own body and mind, the individual is sovereign.[23]

One could assume that this is Mill's final word on this issue. This would be a 'lazy persons reading' of Mill, since if Mill really is wedded to the Harm Principle, it is difficult to understand the rest of this work. What is Mill trying to accomplish in the final four chapters? *On Liberty* becomes particularly difficult on this reading: Why does Mill offer a different version of the Harm Principle here? Is it the same principle? I think that the careful answer is that the version offered in chapter IV is an important improvement on the Harm Principle, but it requires close reading to see why Mill believes it to be so. Why not start with the improved version? Mill wants us to retrace his line of inquiry. He thinks his result is clearer if we follow the process that led him to it.

V. THE LIBERTY PRINCIPLE

One commentator, who actually does read Mill as doing this, is Elizabeth Rapaport in her 'Editor's Introduction' to *On Liberty*. Rapaport finds that in *On Liberty* Mill states 'not one but two principles of demarcation.' The first of these states that the only justification for any social interference in an individual's actions is to prevent that person from doing harm to others. Rapaport calls this 'Principle 1' or the 'Harm-to-Others Principle.' On her account, Mill begins the book by raising Principle 1. He then raises two objections to Principle 1. These two objections cast serious doubts about the efficacy of Principle 1. Mill concedes that, as formulated, this principle simply will not work, and Rapaport notes, he 'puts forward his second principle of demarcation.' Why does Mill do this? Is he simply confused or trying to confuse his audience? Rapaport's answer is a resounding 'no':

> Mill's procedure is a model of open philosophical inquiry. In a way Mill's essay can be regarded as a textbook on how to conduct philosophical inquiry as Mill conceived it, a text that teaches by example, as much as it is a treatise on liberty. Mill is as much or more concerned with enabling his reader to appreciate the problem he is addressing and to engage with him in critical inquiry than in convincing his reader of the truth of his doctrines.[24]

Thus the Harm-to-Others Principle is merely a 'rough first approximation' which Mill will eventually refine into a more accurate and more workable principle. Mill is not trying to sell his readers any particular doctrine of liberty. Rather, he wishes to begin with a carefully and articulately formulated starting point; one that his audience will also find as an extremely important social and political question. He will want to use a method that will allow others to follow his reasoning and then eventually allow others to improve on it. Mill clearly considers himself as progressive and his methodology can be seen as an extension of his commitment to progress. Showing people how to think critically is of much greater importance than telling them what to think. If one really has the right answers, or is open to improvements on one's answers, one should have no fear of a sophisticated audience.

vi. MILL'S DIALECTIC

One aspect of Rapaport's essay that I find striking is that she carries out the above discussion without ever using the word 'dialectic' or any version of it. I think that Mill's methodology in *On Liberty* becomes extremely clear once you add this simple word.

Given Mill's well-known Greco-philia, her omission is particularly surprising. If you start with the assumption that Mill will at times write dialectically then it is not difficult to apply this insight to this work. Mill starts with a thesis that he assumes is familiar enough to his audience. Certainly, some version of the Harm Principle predates Mill. It is clear that von Humbolt explicitly held a version of the harm principle (see the preface to *On Liberty*), and it seems implicitly available in Bentham's 'Offences' (see Chapter 5). But perhaps the most significant historical antecedent is the Declaration of the Rights of Man approved by the National Assembly of France, August 26, 1789. Article 4 reads: 'Liberty consists in the freedom to do everything which injures no one else; hence the exercise of the natural rights of each man has no limits except those which assure to the other members of the society the enjoyment of the same rights. These limits can only be determined by law.' Principle 1, on this account, is the *endoxa*, the opinion of the wise or the many, with which Mill wants to start. However, this thesis, as Mill is quick to note, raises certain problems or puzzles, *aporia*, and thus Principle 1 cries out for reformulation. Let us now read Mill dialectically and see how the central argument of *On Liberty* develops.

Mill offers the Liberty Principle (perhaps, here, it should be referred to as 'the Harm-to-Others Principle') in chapter I of *On Liberty* and raises two objections to it. The first is the problem of externalities: clearly all my actions have some impact on others, and it is quite probable that any action I might take would influence someone adversely. Harm, in this vague sense, cannot be a discriminator between allowable and unallowable conduct. When one takes the last discounted plane ticket or the last seat at a prestigious law school one has harmed, in some real sense, the person who was next in line. But someone will have to be offered the last ticket or the last seat. We live in a world of finite resources. Clearly we will need a method for distinguishing unobjectionable harms from objectionable ones. Second, why should some degree of paternalism not be allowable? Do we really wish to abandon people this severely, never to enter into their sphere to help them? Why would a liberal wish to preclude even a weak form of paternalism? In more modern terms it can be argued that individuals have a right to 'positive liberty' also. They have a right not to be ignored. Ultimately any coherent liberalism, Millian or otherwise, must have a response to these criticisms.

Ultimately I will offer a Millian response to modern opponents of liberalism. Positive liberty is an important topic and any attempt to offer Mill to a modern reader must address the problems it raises for any form of liberalism. But for now I wish to examine the response Mill gives in *On Liberty* to the opponents to be found in his era, that is, the objections from externalities and paternalism. Now these are clearly not creatures of straw; the force of these caused Mill to reformulate his principle in chapter IV. Why does he raise one formulation just to reject it? The answer that I have been suggesting is that this is Mill's version of a dialectic. He formulates, raises objections, and then reformulates. This is, as Rapaport has suggested, a good philosopher offering a model of how to do philosophy well. He works his readers into the philosophic discourse by showing the work he was required to do to get to where he now is. Like a competent logic instructor, he not only provides answers but also a guide for solving problems in general. In the remainder of this section, I will examine how Mill does this.

vii. FREEDOM OF EXPRESSION AND INDIVIDUALITY

One weakness to Rapaport's essay is she does not discuss what Mill attempts to demonstrate in between the first and fourth chapters, or why we should attend to it. Many philosophers could correctly place Mill's well-known argument for free speech in chapter II of *On Liberty*. But many discussions fail to place this argument in the context of the entirety of the main point of *On Liberty*. What is the importance of free speech? It is Mill's clear assertion that facts, evidence, and good arguments do not arise de novo; good arguments do not arise out of nothing.

> But, indeed, the dictum that truth always triumphs over persecution, is one of those pleasant falsehoods which men repeat after one another till they pass into commonplaces, but which all experience refutes. History teems with instances of truth put down by persecution. If not suppressed forever, it may be thrown back for centuries.[25]

Free speech is important because it is through the process of allowing free speech that one most reliably generates the facts, evidence, and good arguments that may lead to truthful opinions. Mill's arguments for this are well known, and frankly, I have little to add to this discussion. The important point is that Mill does argue for the importance to our well-being of allowing an unfettered search for the truth. Mill summarizes his arguments as follows:

> We have now recognized the necessity to the mental well being of mankind (on which all their other well-being depends) of freedom of opinion, and freedom of the expression of opinion, on four distinct grounds; which we will now briefly recapitulate.
>
> First, if any opinion is compelled to silence, that opinion may, for aught we can certainly know, be true. To deny this is to assume our own infallibility.
>
> Secondly, though the silenced opinion be an error, it may, and very commonly does, contain a portion of truth; and since the general or prevailing opinion on any object is rarely or never the whole truth, it is only by the collision of adverse opinions that the remainder of the truth has any chance of being supplied.
>
> Thirdly, even if the received opinion be not only true, but the whole truth; unless it is suffered to be, and actually is, vigorously and earnestly contested, it will, by most of those who receive it, be held in the manner of a prejudice, with little comprehension or feeling of its rational grounds. And not only this, but, fourthly, the meaning of the doctrine itself will be in danger of being lost, or enfeebled, and deprived of its vital effect on the character and conduct: the dogma becoming a mere formal profession, inefficacious for good, but cumbering the ground, and preventing the growth of any real and heartfelt conviction, from reason or personal experience.[26]

Of course, so far I have not argued that a search for the truth is important, since nothing I have argued so far has suggested that the truth is all that important. Perhaps, false beliefs, say, that sacrificing animals to the Water Gods will prevent hurricanes, or that Creation Science is as adequate a theory as Darwinism, or that the Holocaust never occurred, are valuable, if these 'community-supporting' views lead to positive utility. But freedom of opinion, expression, and pursuit of our own conception of the good have another important purpose. Mill suggests that these freedoms are essential for developing our full capacities, and to prevent the development of our full capacities is to deny some important feature of our humanity. Mill writes:

> He who lets the world, or his own portion of it, choose his plan of life for him, has no need of any other faculty than the ape-like one of imitation. He who chooses his plan for himself, employs all his faculties. He must use observation to see, reasoning and judgment to foresee, activity to gather materials for decision, discrimination to decide, and when he has decided, firmness and self-control to hold to his deliberate decision. And these qualities he requires and exercises exactly in proportion as the part of his conduct which he determines according to his own judgment and feelings is a large one. It is possible that he might be guided in some good path, and kept out of harm's way, without any of these things. But what will be his comparative worth as a human being? It really is of importance, not only what men do, but also what manner of men they are that do it. Among the works of man, which human life is rightly employed in perfecting and beautifying, the first in importance surely is man himself. Supposing it were possible to get houses built, corn grown, battles fought, causes tried, and even churches erected and prayers said, by machinery – by automatons in human form – it would be a considerable loss to exchange for these automatons even the men and women who at present inhabit the more civilized parts of the world, and who assuredly are but starved specimens of what nature can and will produce. Human nature is not a machine to be built after a model, and set to do exactly the work prescribed for it, but a tree, which requires to grow and develop itself on all sides, according to the tendency of the inward forces which make it a living thing.[27]

But what is so wrong with such a diminished life? How can a utilitarian argue that the happiness of the individual should be considered paramount? What if it were the case that we could better promote happiness for the community as a whole in many cases, if we lived liked automatons? It is not clear why individuals should not sacrifice their interests for the greater good of society as a whole. It may not be obvious why we should reject the life of imitation out of hand.

viii. THE UTILITY OF EXPERIMENTS IN LIVING

However, it should be clear that the life of imitation is not one that encourages a robust marketplace of ideas. After all, we will not have a rich debate on the issues of the day if everyone is a product of, and offers a recitation of, the status quo. We would even have a radically diminished debate if relatively few individuals are encouraged to develop their individual capacities. Even if many of us choose the life of imitation, it would be important to make it possible for others to reject this path. We would need role models. Even if we should wish to copy our book of life from manuscripts of greater geniuses, we should encourage the flourishing of such geniuses. Mill writes:

> I insist thus emphatically on the importance of genius, and the necessity of allowing it to unfold itself freely both in thought and in practice, being well aware that no one will deny the position in theory, but knowing also that almost every one, in reality, is totally indifferent to it. People think genius a fine thing if it enables a man to write an exciting poem, or paint a picture. But in its true sense, that of originality in thought and action, though no one says that it is not a thing to be admired, nearly all, at heart, think they can do very well without it. Unhappily this is too natural to be wondered at. Originality is the one thing which unoriginal minds cannot feel the use of. They cannot see what it is to do for them: how should they? If they could see what it would do for them, it would not be originality. The first service which originality has to render them, is that of opening their eyes: which being once fully done, they would have a chance of being themselves original. Meanwhile, recollecting that nothing was ever yet done which some one was not the first to do, and that all good things which exist are the fruits of originality, let them be modest enough to believe that there is something still left for it to accomplish, and assure themselves that they are more in need of originality, the less they are conscious of the want.[28]

Thus, even those who wish to lead a life of imitation should be willing to accept the need for others to reject it; if for no other reason than to offer themselves a multiplicity of lives of imitation. If no one experiments with their life, if no one is encouraged to find their own way, even those who have no desire to do so will be diminished. But a free marketplace of ideas depends on the willingness of many to engage in experiments in living. Without an acceptance of allowing others to engage in robust exploration of various experiments in living, we are unlikely to develop those unique perspectives that push the envelope, rock the boat, or upset the applecart. Today's cranks, kooks, and misfits may well contribute nothing to today's debate. But as Mill argues, it will be hard to know this in advance of allowing them their experiments in living. But if we shut down these experiments today, we will never know if they could contribute something to tomorrow's debate. Yesterday's cranks, kooks, and misfits may well turn out to be today's eccentrics, and some of today's eccentrics may well be tomorrow's geniuses. Mill writes:

> In this age the mere example of non-conformity, the mere refusal to bend the knee to custom, is itself a service. Precisely because the tyranny of opinion is such as to make eccentricity a reproach, it is desirable, in order to break through that tyranny, that people should be eccentric. Eccentricity has always abounded when and where strength of character has abounded; and the amount of eccentricity in a society has generally been proportional to the amount of genius, mental vigor, and moral courage which it contained. That so few now dare to be eccentric, marks the chief danger of the time.[29]

There are obvious costs to being eccentric; after all, by definition, others will often find you eccentric. But Mill suggests that our eccentrics perform for us an essential service. They are willing to take on a hostile society in the hope of discovering something meaningful beyond the status quo. As many conservatives are more than willing to tell us, most of these new ideas, opinions, and experiments in life turn out worse than the old ones, and, thus, our eccentrics are likely to fail. But this does not mean that they do not provide a useful service. The eccentrics offer their own lives as experiments in living in order to further the goal of creation of new role models, new ideas, new opinions, and new experiments in living. Ultimately, they provide the essential service of furthering our search for lives that are truly worth living. But it should be noted that Mill finds a clear connection between the search for a life that is worth living, and a search for the truth. He writes:

> There are, it is alleged, certain beliefs, so useful, not to say indispensable to well-being, that it is as much the duty of governments

> to uphold those beliefs, as to protect any other of the interests of society. In a case of such necessity, and so directly in the line of their duty, something less than infallibility may, it is maintained, warrant, and even bind, governments, to act on their own opinion, confirmed by the general opinion of mankind. It is also often argued, and still oftener thought, that none but bad men would desire to weaken these salutary beliefs; and there can be nothing wrong, it is thought, in restraining bad men, and prohibiting what only such men would wish to practise. This mode of thinking makes the justification of restraints on discussion not a question of the truth of doctrines, but of their usefulness; and flatters itself by that means to escape the responsibility of claiming to be an infallible judge of opinions. But those who thus satisfy themselves, do not perceive that the assumption of infallibility is merely shifted from one point to another. The usefulness of an opinion is itself matter of opinion: as disputable, as open to discussion and requiring discussion as much, as the opinion itself. There is the same need of an infallible judge of opinions to decide an opinion to be noxious, as to decide it to be false, unless the opinion condemned has full opportunity of defending itself. And it will not do to say that the heretic may be allowed to maintain the utility or harmlessness of his opinion, though forbidden to maintain its truth. The truth of an opinion is part of its utility.[30]

Thus, there is a clear connection between our search for a life worth living, those views that are essential for our well-being, and a search for the truth. If the truth of an opinion is part of its utility, and we can find the truth of this opinion only in a free marketplace of ideas, then utilitarianism clearly must support a free marketplace of ideas. But a truly vigorous marketplace of ideas – one that is capable of discovering new truths about matters as fundamental as what models we should use to structure our own lives – must let eccentrics and their experiments in living flourish.

To summarize, I take what Mill wishes to accomplish in the second and third chapters of *On Liberty* to be a reasonably straightforward and valid argument. If we want a society that is capable of a meaningful search for the truth, we want a society in which there is a rich and robust marketplace of ideas. If we want a society in which there is a rich and robust marketplace of ideas, we must encourage eccentrics and their experiments in living. Thus, if we want a society that is capable of a meaningful search for the truth, we must encourage eccentrics and their experiments in living. But if the liberal utilitarian considers this argument to be sound, the need for a sphere of private morality where one can engage in one's own experiment in living seems clear. It should now prove possible to see what Mill wishes to accomplish in chapter IV.

ix. THE FINAL FORMULATION OF THE LIBERTY PRINCIPLE

Mill's clear and unequivocal purpose in *On Liberty* is 'to make the fitting adjustment between individual independence and social control.' He begins his reformulation of the Liberty Principle in chapter IV by introducing a distinction between self-regarding and other-regarding behavior.

> Each will receive its proper share if each has that which more particularly concerns it. To individuality should belong the part of life in which it is chiefly the individual that is interested; to society the part which chiefly interests society.[31]

Mill thinks that since we all receive the protection of society we have two basic obligations to society; we must respect the rights of others that are members of our society and help maintain the defense of our society from outsiders.[32] Mill does not find that his society is based on a social contract; but, to the extent that we live in a society, we owe these minimal duties to it. To this extent our actions are other-regarding. Mill draws the line between self-regarding and other-regarding conduct by distinguishing between conduct that shows a defect of 'prudence or personal dignity' and conduct that acts as an 'offense against the rights of others.' What makes this first group of cases self-regarding is they do not involve any 'distinct and assignable obligations to others.' We draw this distinction by looking at who bears the brunt of the consequences.

Normally, one should be allowed to spend one's money as one wishes, but parents who foolishly spend their money and neglect their children's education have violated an obligation to them. Similarly, one should be allowed to decide one's own consumption of alcohol but a military officer who is drunk on duty is unable to fulfill his or her obligations to the public. These are examples, given by Mill, of conduct that while normally self-regarding and thus allowable has become other-regarding. The key here is that we can find either a 'perceptible hurt' to an 'assignable individual' or a 'specific duty' to the public. In the cases I referred to earlier, taking the last discounted plane ticket or the last seat in a prestigious law school, it is clear that in some meaningful sense I have harmed the next person in line. But in most cases I will not have any clear and assignable obligation to relinquish my opportunity to the next person in line, and I clearly will not under normal circumstances violate their rights by exercising my options. Perhaps Mill's clearest attempt to define 'rights' is found in this passage from *Utilitarianism*:

> When we call anything a person's right, we mean that he has a valid claim on society to protect him in the possession of it, either by the force of law, or by that of education and opinion. If he has what we consider a sufficient claim, on whatever account, to have something guaranteed to him by society, we say that he has a right to it. If we desire to prove that anything does not belong to him by right, we think this done as soon as it is admitted that society ought not to take measures for securing it to him, but should leave him to chance, or to his own exertions. Thus, a person is said to have a right to what he can earn in fair professional competition, because society ought not to allow any other person to hinder him from endeavoring to earn in that manner as much as he can. But he has not a right to three hundred a year, though he may happen to be earning it; because society is not called on to provide that he shall earn that sum. On the contrary, if he owns ten thousand pounds three per cent stock, he has a right to three hundred a-year because society has come under an obligation to provide him with an income of that amount . . . To have a right, then, is, I conceive, to have something which society ought to defend me in the possession of. If the objector goes on to ask, why it ought? I can give him no other reason than general utility.[33]

The point is that once we move away from talk about 'harm' to talk about 'rights and obligations' we have a fairly clear understanding of when and under what circumstances society will be warranted in interfering with the actions of an individual. The problem with the Harm Principle is that it puts too great a burden on the actor; you never really know when you are harming someone, and whether this harm is objectionable or not. It should be much clearer, however, to recognize when you are violating another's rights or ignoring clear and assignable obligations. We can recognize when a breach of trust or other issues of fidelity are involved. But there are two other reasons, according to Mill, why we should not allow the problem of externalities to prevent individual liberty. The first is that one does not usually inspire bad conduct by example. If the conduct really is bad then invariably 'the example on the whole is more salutary than hurtful.' Bad conduct will usually lead to bad consequences; the result will have an educational effect on the public at large. Second, a certain amount of bad conduct will arise in any pluralistic society. But this amount of bad conduct 'society can afford to bear for the sake of the greater good of human freedom.'

Mill also thinks his reformulated principle can withstand the objections raised from paternalism and positive liberty. There are two important objections that Mill will need to be able to respond to. The first is that freedom, in any meaningful sense, seems to incorporate more than free choice. It is also essential that one have reasonable alternatives from which to choose. The second is that really essential freedoms are not likely to be completely self-regarding. Freedom to worship, freedom of occupation, and many recreational freedoms can only be undertaken in a societal context.

Mill is clearly worried about these issues. He recognizes the social nature of human existence. He thinks that 'human beings owe to each other help to distinguish the better from the worse' but he argues that this is a duty to persuade rather than coerce. Society, armed with the 'power of education,' public opinion, and 'natural penalties' (the usual suffering that comes from violating societal norms), will certainly have an influence on the behavior of all members of society. Our social nature will guarantee it. We exist as social creatures and we will be strongly influenced by the type of society in which we live. Armed with all this power, society needs go no further. Not only should society refrain from going further than this; but, more basically as a simple psychological fact, it will fail when it attempts to go further than this. Coercion, as our current and previous attempts at drug and alcohol prohibition demonstrate, does not often work, or, minimally, will prove extremely costly. Prudence and temperance cannot be forced on individuals; they will naturally rebel. Society can also never know the individual as well as the individual does. The individual is the person most likely to know her or his own case. The individual will know his or her own interests and motivations. Finally, in what Mill thinks is his strongest point, society is likely to interfere wrongly and in the wrong place.

> But the strongest of all the arguments against the interference of the public with purely personal conduct, is that when it does interfere, the odds are that it interferes wrongly, and in the wrong place. On questions of social morality, of duty to others, the opinion of the public, that is, of an overruling majority, though often wrong, is likely to be still oftener right; because on such questions they are only required to judge of their own interests; of the manner in which some mode of conduct, if allowed to be practised, would affect themselves. But the opinion of a similar majority, imposed as a law on the minority, on questions of self-regarding conduct, is quite as likely to be wrong as right; for in these cases public opinion means, at the best, some people's opinion of what is good or bad for other people; while very often it does not even mean that; the public, with the most perfect indifference, passing over the pleasure or convenience of those whose conduct they censure, and considering only their own preference. There are many who consider as an injury to themselves any conduct which they have a distaste for, and resent it as an outrage to their feelings; as a religious bigot, when charged with disregarding the religious feelings of others, has been known to retort that they disregard his feelings, by persisting in their abominable worship or creed. But there is no parity between the feeling of a person for his own opinion, and the feeling of another who is offended at his holding it; no more than between the desire of a thief to take a purse, and the desire of the right owner to keep it. And a person's taste is as much his own peculiar concern as his opinion or his purse.

The majority does a good job of deciding 'questions of social morality' and 'duty to others', but in self-regarding cases society is 'quite as likely to be wrong as right.' People will often find 'an injury to themselves in conduct they have a distaste for.' Unchecked, this would allow majorities to enforce their own mere preferences on minorities. But still, it seems possible to question why Mill is justified in preventing paternalistic actions to such a great degree, and how this is consistent with his utilitarianism. A superficial reading of Mill could turn his philosophy into an armchair activity for ivory tower intellectuals. Mill needs a morality that will allow his strong confidence in individuals to be compatible with other utilitarian goals; he needs a well-formulated moral theory to back up his notion of freedom. Mill, in my opinion has done this but one must examine Mill's liberalism in light of his utilitarian ethics carefully to find it. To this I now turn my attention.

CHAPTER 4

MILL'S MINIMALIST UTILITARIANISM

i. MILL'S MINIMALIST ETHICS

Since the usual reading of Mill as a maximizing act-utilitarian, as illustrated by James Rachels and others, seems fraught with difficulties, I will consider other readings of Mill.[1] One way to avoid these difficulties is offered by Rem B. Edwards. Similar interpretations of Mill may be found in the writings of D. G. Brown and David Lyons. These commentators, unlike Edwards, do not use the term 'minimizing utilitarian.' Their contributions to this interpretation of Mill will be explored in more detail later in this chapter. I will use the term 'minimizing utilitarianism' to refer to Edwards' theory and his interpretation of Mill. I prefer the term 'minimalist utilitarianism' since it lacks optimific connotations which seem to confuse some readers.

According to Edwards, Mill was not a maximizing act-utilitarian; he was a minimizing utilitarian. Minimizing utilitarianism, while still a consequentialist theory, is radically distinct from act- or rule-utilitarianism. It should be noted that many commentators use the term 'consequentialist' to imply maximization.[2] I will use the term in its wider sense; a consequentialist theory is merely one that judges the rightness or wrongness of acts by evaluating their consequences.

Both act- and rule-utilitarians are maximizing consequentialists for whom the correctness of actions or rules is determined by evaluating whether the largest possible utility or the smallest possible disutility results. They disagree about the processes that produce maximum possible utility. The act-utilitarian claims that this must be decided on a case-by-case basis, and the rule-utilitarian believes that it is best achieved by following those specific rules which would maximize utility if everyone acted upon them. In either case the utilitarian's duty to maximize utility is the fundamental moral principle that overrides all other moral considerations. Since Mill is commonly read as a maximizing utilitarian I wish to accomplish three goals in this chapter. First, I will present Edwards' reading of Mill. Secondly, I will offer some of my own modifications and clarifications to this reading. Thirdly, I will marshal evidence against reading Mill as a maximizing utilitarian, and for reading Mill as a moral minimalist.

ii. EDWARDS' READING OF MILL

Rem B. Edwards has argued that Mill is not a standard act- or rule-utilitarian. Rather Edwards suggests that:

> Mill's utilitarianism was actually a minimizing utilitarianism which claims only that we are morally obligated to abstain from inflicting harm, to actively prevent harm, to actively provide for all persons or sentient beings certain *minimal* essentials of any sort of positive well being whatsoever, such as life, liberty, security, individuality and self-determination, food and shelter, basic education, equal opportunity to pursue happiness, etc., and beyond that to exercise a decent minimum of charity.[3]

This differs from, say, Richard Brandt's version of rule-utilitarianism (Ideal Utilitarianism) in that Brandt would not limit himself to these criteria for moral obligation, since the ideal rules might suggest otherwise. According to Edwards, Mill's minimizing utilitarianism does not make a fundamental moral principle out of the principle of utility. Mill's minimizing utilitarianism merely affirms that it would be *desirable* to maximize happiness for the greatest number, but not that we are morally *required* to do so. Rather than being the fundamental principle of Mill's moral philosophy, the Principle of Utility really is better thought of as the 'first axiom' of 'general axiology' or what Mill termed 'the Art of Life.' The Art of Life has 'three departments, Morality, Prudence or policy, and Aesthetics; the Right, the expedient, and the Beautiful.'[4] According to Edwards, Mill held that 'moral right and wrong, moral rules, moral obligation, and moral virtue' can be identified by reference to promoting happiness, '*but the reference is clearly not one of simple identity*.'

> Supplemental considerations are required to mark out the province of the moral and distinguish it from the provinces of prudence, aesthetic taste, politics, etc., all of which also have the Principle of Utility as their proper 'foundation' or 'criterion.' None of them have it without qualifications as their inherent first principle, however. Additional conceptual features must be introduced to differentiate the first principle of general axiology from the first principles of the provinces thereof.[5]

Edwards also notes that the province of the moral must then be distinguished from non-moral domains of value such as prudence, aesthetic taste, politics and law. Moral duties are distinguished from non-moral ones by two important supplemental considerations: First, moral duties must be worth the cost of social enforcement, which always has costs. Thus duties are morally obligatory only if their observance will result in value greater than the cost of enforcing them. Whether individuals are sanctioned through inculcating guilty consciences, social condemnation, or the civil and criminal penalties of the state, moral duties are only those that are worth the cost of enforcement. Secondly, these moral duties must be correlatable with rules for moral action that are easily taught and learned. Rules become very important under this system, but there is a clear distinction between Mill's utilitarianism and rule-utilitarianism. Rule-utilitarianism affirms that moral rules are justified if everyone's following them would have the best consequences. The minimalist utilitarian rejects this and considers the costs of implementing and enforcing moral rules as general social practices. Under minimalist utilitarianism, acts are morally wrong only when they violate 'a moral rule that is worth the cost of being instituted and enforced as a general social practice.'[6] Thus, many desirable acts are not morally obligatory. In fact few desirable acts would meet the standards of moral obligation:

> The costs of initiating, teaching, and enforcing these sanctions have to be taken into account in determining which acts are to count as morally obligatory. Once these costs are counted, Mill was convinced that only a relatively few desirable acts can be classified as moral obligations, i.e. as acts that society justifiably could coercively require of its members. Other desirable acts fall into non-moral domains such as those of manners, aesthetic

> tastes, prudential well being or expediency, exalted heroism, and saintly sacrifice.[7]

Only those desirable kinds of acts that are worth the price of initiating, teaching and enforcing become moral rules. Saintliness is an admirable quality, but to require sainthood of everyone as does maximizing act-utilitarianism would be absurd. The price associated with creating and maintaining such a state of affairs would be prohibitive.

What then is morally required? Restrained by enforceability and teachability, as just explained, the principle of utility will help us to develop a set of 'concrete action guiding rules' that are worth the price of initiating, teaching, and enforcing. The basic norm of morality then becomes:

> To the extent that the results are possible, we are morally required to act in accord with those concrete secondary rules which demand (a) that we avoid harm to all other persons (or sentient beings) who are affected by our behavior and (b) that we protect and/or provide for everyone else (or every other sentient being certain minimal essential conditions of any sort of well being whatsoever, such as life, liberty, security, basic education, and basic health, and (c) that we engage in a decent minimum of charity or benevolence (and perhaps other 'imperfect obligations' such as gratitude).[8]

Edwards and Graber are borrowing the perfect/imperfect distinction from Kant. An imperfect obligation is one where a person is obliged to perform a certain action but not to any particular individual. For example, if I owe Jones five dollars, I have a perfect obligation to repay Jones. However, even though I have an imperfect duty to be charitable, I have no duty to give money to Planned Parenthood (assuming that I do agree with their goals) – I may prefer to give my money to the ACLU.

Thus, minimalist utilitarianism provides a solid ground for moral rights. Those secondary rules that are worth their associated costs place moral claims upon us. As Edwards sees it, we violate another's rights when we ignore those moral rules that prevent: (a) harming others, and (b) ignoring minimally essential conditions for well being. Justice becomes the main component of moral obligation; it 'consists in those perfect duties that protect and provide moral rights for everyone on every relevant occasion.'[9]

iii. A POINT OF CLARIFICATION

Before attempting to justify Edwards' reading of Mill, I wish to suggest why I think it is an important one to examine. In general, consequentialist moral theories can differ radically in how demanding they are. Standard versions of act- and rule-utilitarianism are often very demanding. Brandt's Ideal utilitarism is less so. Brandt suggests modifying standard rule-utilitarianism in two ways. First, he would agree with Edwards that moral rules should be easily taught, and worth the cost of enforcement. Secondly, he believes that the ideal set of rules should be the ones that would maximize happiness if they were accepted and generally followed by roughly ninety percent of the population. Thus, one is only morally required to contribute one's fair share; for example, the duty to feed the homeless requires that one's contribution be large enough to insure that all the homeless were fed, if others meet their obligations as well. Edwards wishes to lower the demands further by suggesting that our fair share would not maximize the good, but rather minimize harm.[10] Thus, Edwards is attempting to develop a less onerous utilitarianism that still maintains some of utilitarianism's attractive features.

In the previous chapters I have suggested that if Mill was a not a maximizing utilitarian then it would be possible to reconcile Mill's liberalism with his consequentialist morality. It would then be possible to use this full-blooded Mill to construct a theory of justice. Mill is, however, commonly read as a maximizing utilitarian. In light of this fact, I wish to accomplish four purposes in the remainder of this chapter. First, I wish to suggest why so many readings of Mill are wrong. Secondly, I will demonstrate that Mill is not an ethical extremist. Moreover, if one takes Mill's liberalism seriously, the consistent reading suggests that Mill is a moral minimalist. Thirdly, I will provide a detailed account of Mill's axiology and show that this allows reading Mill as a minimalist utilitarian. Fourthly, I will show the importance that Mill placed on self-development and the formation of character, and how this reinforces reading Mill as a minimizing utilitarian.

iv. PHILOSOPHY AND FASHION

Philosophy, like any other human endeavor, has its fads and fashions. There are eras where philosophy is revered and philosophers are heroes. The medieval church endowed Augustine, Anselm, and Aquinas with sainthood. Early twentieth-century America considered John Dewey and William James among its public intellectuals. The French made Jean-Paul Sartre a major figure in their culture. However, American culture as we find it today is less than friendly to philosophy. There is currently no demand for philosophers to enter the public debate; and, with the possible exception of John Rawls, there are no twentieth-century American philosophers who have made a major impact on the contemporary political debate.

Even academic philosophy has its fashion statements. During the Middle Ages the scholastics singled out Aristotle as beyond comparison; he was simply 'the philosopher.' During the Enlightenment, he was denounced as a hopelessly dogmatic essentialist whose views were antithetical to the new evolving scientific picture of the world. Only in the last hundred years has Aristotle received the charitable reading that a philosopher of his enormous abilities deserves. But Aristotle still is tarnished because his views are associated with a dogmatic scholastic Christianity. The way Aristotle was interpreted for hundreds of years still affects the way Aristotle is interpreted today.

Aristotle also suffers from having been so influential for so long. Postmodernists reject essentialism so passionately that one would almost assume something personal is at stake; after all, no one would seriously argue that there are no universal features of human existence. We all die, right? A new generation of philosophers tends to wish to distance themselves from their elders, particularly when their elders have achieved great distinction. Why else would America today have so few Dewey scholars? Why would so many American bookstores be stocked with obscure continental postmodernists, and be devoid of the works of major Anglo-American thinkers such as Dewey, James, Russell, Bentham, and the Mills?

In an era when philosophers have such a small influence upon public debate, it is hard to understand how influential Mill was in his own day. Perhaps the only philosopher whose specter looms as large over the twentieth century is Karl Marx. In a century that has been dominated by Marxism, however, it is hard to realize how obscure Marx was during the period of Mill's greatest influence. As Thomas Sowell wrote in 1985:

> Marx's legendary fame today makes it difficult to realize that he was an obscure figure with no substantial following in the early 1860s, that his writings were largely ignored, and that even a man as knowledgeable as John Stuart Mill could live for twenty years in the same city, writing on the same topics, in utter ignorance that someone named Karl Marx existed.[11]

Sowell's choice of Mill in this regard is far from accidental. Mill was as famous during his life as Marx was obscure. The year 1848 was an important year for what was then known as political economy. It was the year Marx and Engels published *The Communist Manifesto*, and Mill published his *Principles of Political Economy*. By the early 1860s Mill's *Principles* had gone into multiple editions and was widely regarded as the definitive work on political economy. During his lifetime Mill was considered a great thinker in this field, and Marx was virtually unknown. It is one of those remarkable reversals of fortunes in intellectual history that these roles would be reversed in such a short period of time. Today Marx is either famous or infamous, depending upon your political views, as an economic thinker. One practically has to be a Mill scholar to know that such a view was held about Mill a hundred or so years ago.

So, as we have seen, the curtain rises and falls on philosophical fashion. By 1950 Marxism and various responses to Marxism dominated world thought. Marxism was such a powerful force that, in reaction to the perceived threat posed by Communism, a country founded on constitutionally guaranteed rights would allow a demagogue like McCarthy to violate egregiously the civil liberties of its citizens. Senator Joseph McCarthy (Republican, Wisconsin) gained prominence in 1950 charging that the State department was infested with Communists. Today 'McCarthyism' is a term of derision applied to those who supposedly have engaged in reckless or indiscriminate charges of political disloyalty. On the other hand, in 1950 one might have asked: 'John Stuart who?'

v. URMSON'S REEXAMINATION

Perhaps the tide began to turn for Mill in the 1950s. In 1953 J.O. Urmson wrote an influential article that began a reexamination of Mill's ethical philosophy. Urmson began with a scathing denunciation of the Mill scholarship of his day:

> It is a matter which should be of great interest to those who study the psychology of philosophers that the theories of some great philosophers of the past are studied with the most patient and accurate scholarship, while those of others are so burlesqued and travestied by critics and commentators that it is hard to believe that their works are ever seriously read with a sympathetic interest, or even that they are read at all. Amongst those who suffer most in this way John Stuart Mill is an outstanding example . . . even more perplexing is the almost universal misconstruction placed upon Mill's ethical doctrines; for his *Utilitarianism* is a work which every undergraduate is set to read and which one would therefore expect Mill's critics to have read at least once. But this, apparently, is not so; and instead of Mill's own doctrines a travesty is discussed, so the most common criticisms of him are simply irrelevant . . . [If Mill was interpreted with] half the sympathy automatically accorded to Plato, Leibniz, and Kant an essentially consistent thesis can be discovered which is very superior to that usually attributed to Mill and immune to the common run of criticisms.[12]

Urmson finds Mill read incorrectly in primarily two ways. First, he is read as an ethical naturalist who defined 'rightness in terms of the natural consequences of actions,' or alternately Mill is read as suggesting that an act is right if 'it promotes the ultimate end better than any alternative, and otherwise it is wrong.'[13] According to Urmson, if this were the case then Mill's work 'would indeed be fit for little more than the halting eristic of philosophical infants.'[14] The second view above, as Urmson suggests, was the dominant view about Mill at the time Urmson wrote, and I have shown in the previous chapters that it still surfaces in commonly accepted introductory texts today. To put this view in more modern terms, Mill is a maximizing act-utilitarian. Urmson, as previously noted, finds this interpretation fatally flawed, and offers the following set of four propositions as a first step in a reasonable exegesis of Mill's moral philosophy instead:

A. A particular action is justified as being right by showing that it is in accord with some moral rule. It is shown to be wrong by showing that it transgresses some moral rule.
B. A moral rule is shown to be correct by showing that the recognition of the rule promotes the ultimate end.
C. Moral rules can be justified only in regard to matters in which the general welfare is more than negligibly effected.
D. Where no moral rule is applicable the question of the rightness or wrongness of particular acts does not arise, though the worth of actions can be estimated in different ways.[15]

Urmson claims that this is no more than 'a skeleton plan' for Mill's account in *Utilitarianism*, and that Mill 'puts the matter more richly and more subtly in his book.'[16] However, I think that there are at least three insightful points that come from Urmson's discussion.

First, Urmson recognizes the importance of rules (what Mill usually calls secondary principles) for Mill's moral philosophy. Secondly, many actions fall outside of the moral domain. These actions only affect the general good negligibly. Thirdly, some non-moral acts are capable of being evaluated.

vi. THE DIFFICULTY WITH THE MAXIMIZING READING

Urmson's article provoked a great debate in the philosophic community: Is Mill a rule-utilitarian or is he an act-utilitarian?[17] But phrasing the debate this way misses much of what should be Urmson's point. Both rule- and act-utilitarians are maximizing utilitarians. No maximizing utilitarian would accept that morality only concerns 'matters in which the general welfare is more than negligibly affected.' Mill in *Utilitarianism* makes this point so explicitly and so clearly it is hard to believe, as Urmson has noted, that Mill's critics have actually bothered to read him. Mill clearly rejected the ethical extremist position. Mill actually believes that our opportunities to act in a manner in which the general welfare is more than negligibly affected are quite rare. In answering the charge that utilitarianism would require us to 'always act from the inducement of promoting the general interests of society' Mill in *Utilitarianism* writes:

> The multiplication of happiness is, according to the utilitarian ethics, the object of virtue: the occasions on which any person

> (except one in a thousand) has it in his power to do this on an extended scale, in other words to be a public benefactor, are but exceptional; and on these occasions alone is he called on to consider public utility; in every other case, private utility, the interest or happiness of some few persons, is all he has to attend to.[18]

One wonders what those who hold the view that Mill is a maximizing utilitarian make of such a passage. Why would it be plausible to suggest that an ethical extremist thinks that for most of us our opportunities to act from duty are exceptional, and in any case, would only apply to one person in a thousand? What could an ethical extremist possibly mean by 'private utility,' and why would an ethical extremist wish to suggest that in most cases public utility should be ignored in favor of private utility? In any case, the ethical extremist owes us a rather sophisticated theory of human psychology that would justify such an account. If we are morally required as the ethical extremist suggests, say, not to simply feed all the hungry peoples of the Third World, but provide them with a standard of living that maximizes utility, would this not require most Americans to radically change their behavior? To suggest that we could simply go forward without virtually every American being morally required radically to adjust their behavior, in my view, would be not taking ethical extremism seriously.

vii. THE MINIMALIST READING

Two possible answers suggest themselves. Those that hold what Urmson calls the 'received view' simply treat such a passage as an aberration. Mill, on their account, is simply sloppy and inconsistent. The more plausible interpretation is that the received view treats prudential choices as moral choices; but, as noted by Louis P. Pojman, Mill's utilitarianism (along with Hobbesian contractarianism and most deontological ethics) 'tends to be minimalist' calling on us to adhere to a core of necessary rules (e.g., do not steal, harm, murder, or lie) in order for society to function. The accent is on *social control*: Morality is largely preventive, safeguarding rights and moral space where people may carry out their projects unhindered by the intrusions of others.[19] Pojman wishes to distinguish between the 'weak' form of Mill's utilitarianism and the 'strong' form found in the work of Peter Singer. Strong utilitarians place most of life under the strict scrutiny of morality. For the strong utilitarian, if we were able to prevent anything with negative consequences from happening without sacrificing something of equal or greater worth we would be required to do so. Of course, it goes without saying that this places the bulk of our lives in the moral domain. Our duties to positively help those less fortunate than ourselves would be overwhelming. A 'weak' utilitarianism, on Pojman's account, opens up a large domain of what is morally permissible; we are allowed a large area of morally neutral space in which to chart our own self-development. But this desire for a moral free space in which to cultivate our personality, desires, talents, and abilities is at the very core of liberalism. As Will Kymlicka puts it, the liberal desires to live life from the inside – free to 'form, revise, and act upon our plans of life.'[20] The freedom to form and revise our own life projects, to be the person in charge of who we are, is crucial for the liberal. The connection between the liberal and the moral minimalist is quite clear in Daniel Callahan's characterization of the moral minimalist position:

> It has been one that stressed the transcendence of the individual over the community, the need to tolerate all moral viewpoints, the autonomy of the self as the highest human good, the informed consent contract as the model of human relationships. We are obliged under the most generous reading of a minimalist ethic only to honor our voluntarily undertaken family obligations, to keep our promises, and to respect contracts freely entered into with other freely consenting adults. Beyond those minimal standards, we are free to do as we like, guided by nothing other than our private standards of good and evil.[21]

In this passage, Callahan describes a moral minimalist ethic. But it could easily be construed as a description of a liberal world-view. The autonomy that is stressed by Callahan is a distinctly liberal one. Freedom is the negative freedom to do as we like once those obligations that we have voluntarily entered into are met, but Callahan omits Mill's emphasis on the necessity for respecting basic human rights whether we have voluntarily chosen to do so or not. Perhaps it would be rash to suggest that all moral minimalists must be liberals; but clearly if Callahan's characterization is correct, moral minimalism is compatible with liberalism.

The virtue of reading Mill as a moral minimalist who emphasizes justice is readily apparent. When Mill is read as an ethical extremist there is an incredible tension between Mill's ethics and his liberalism. But moral minimalism as characterized by Pojman and Callahan fits liberalism like a tailor-made suit.

The questions are then simple: Is there textual support for reading Mill this way? Is there sufficient evidence that Mill was a moral minimalist? Does this evidence compare favorably with evidence that Mill is a moral maximalist? Is Mill's moral minimalism compatible with his utilitarianism? I will show that it is possible to answer all of these questions affirmatively.

viii. MILL AND MORAL EXTREMISM

I have already suggested that a close reading of *Utilitarianism* causes difficulties for the received view that reads Mill as a moral extremist. A moral extremist such as Shelly Kagan would hardly suggest that nine hundred and ninety-nine individuals out of a thousand, even in Mill's era, would not have the opportunity to more than negligibly affect the common good. Kagan has characterized moral extremism as follows:

> Morality requires that you perform – of those acts not otherwise forbidden – that act which can be reasonably expected to lead to the best consequences overall . . . If this claim is correct, most of my actions are *immoral*, for almost *nothing* that I do makes optimal use of my time and resources . . . few of us believe this claim and none of us live in accordance with it.[22]

For Kagan an important question is whether utilitarianism is too demanding. If utilitarians are required to live in accordance with this formulation of consequentialism, utilitarianism would certainly be a very demanding ethical philosophy. One might legitimately ask whether all maximizing utilitarians would assent to this formulation of consequentialism. Following Kagan, I will refer to a supporter of Kagan's moral extremism as 'the Extremist.'[23]

Mill was no fan of the Extremist. He makes this perfectly clear in his *Later Speculations of M. Comte*. Comte, according to Mill, was a 'morality intoxicated man.' 'Every question to him is a matter of morality, and no motive but that of morality is permitted.'[24] The

Extremist has a similar addiction. As Kagan notes, if the Extremist were to go to the movies, he or she would be guilty of a breach of morality. The time could be better spent caring for the sick or elderly. The money could be spent on famine relief.[25] For the Extremist the simplest daily activity becomes a major moral decision. Any indulgence beyond what is necessary for survival becomes immoral. But Mill clearly rejects this position when he finds it in Comte. Furthermore, he rejects it in a context where he explicitly states that utilitarians, for the most part, would not accept it either. Mill writes:

> [According to Comte] we should endeavor to starve the whole of the desires which point to our personal satisfactions, by denying them all gratifications not strictly required by physical necessities. The golden rule of morality [for Comte] is to live for others . . . To do as we would be done by, and to love our neighbor as ourself are not sufficient for him: they partake, he thinks, of the nature of personal calculations. We should endeavor not to love ourselves at all.[26]

Mill clearly suggests that the Extremist's morality is deficient in a crucial aspect of any worthwhile moral theory: A worthwhile moral theory provides a foundation for a life that is worth living. The extremist's life is one devoid of personal satisfaction. It is a life of almost total abnegation. Mill must reject such a theory. Utilitarianism is at some level, after all, about happiness; and however one wishes to define happiness, it is impossible to be happy without loving oneself at least a little. Mill wants a society that makes as many people happy as is possible, not one that demands that none of them is.

Mill also thinks that the Extremist errs in the belief that there are no supererogatory acts. Extremists may have choices between acts, of course; but they must always choose to act in a way that produces the best consequences. For Mill, the class of morally virtuous acts is much larger than the class of morally obligatory acts. There is a large class of acts that are morally virtuous and worth doing, but are not morally obligatory. Once again, we are allowed a large area of moral permissibility in which to chart our own self-development. It is desirable, of course, to encourage ourselves and others to perform acts of supererogation; such conduct is morally desirable, but not morally obligatory. Mill clearly believes that an act of supererogation falls beyond the call of moral duty and should be done voluntarily. According to Mill, all Extremists like Comte are guilty of the same error. They make:

> [T]he same ethical mistake as the theory of Calvinism, that every act in life should be done for the glory of God, and whatever is not duty is a sin. It does not perceive that between the region of duty and that of sin there is an intermediate space, the region of positive worthiness. It is not good that persons should be bound, by other people's opinion, to do everything that they would deserve praise for doing. There is a standard of altruism to which all should be required to come up, and a degree beyond it which is not obligatory, but meritorious. It is incumbent on everyone to restrain the pursuit of his personal objects within the limits consistent with the essential interests of others. What those limits are, it is the province of ethical science to determine; and to keep all individuals and aggregations of individuals within them, is the proper office of punishment and of moral blame.[27]

For Mill it is clear that there is room in morality for people to live virtuous or even heroic lives, but it is important that no one is compelled to do so by the moral sanction of law, public opinion, or private conscience. There are minimal demands that society can make on everyone, for example, not to harm others or violate contractual agreements. We should praise and reward those who are extremely altruistic. We should teach our children to both be charitable and to have the greatest admiration for such altruists. In this way, Mill believes, we will obtain a society in which it is possible for human beings to flourish, and to construct lives that are worth living.

> As a rule of conduct, to be enforced by moral sanctions, we think no more should be attempted than to prevent people from doing harm to others, or omitting to do such good as they have undertaken. Demanding no more than this, society, in any tolerable circumstances, obtains much more; for the natural activity of human nature, shut out from all noxious directions, will expand itself in useful ones. This is our conception of the moral rule prescribed by the religion of Humanity. But above this standard there is an unlimited range of moral worth, up to the most exalted heroism, which should be fostered by every positive

> encouragement, though not converted into an obligation. It is as much a part of our scheme as of M. Comte's, that the direct cultivation of altruism, and the subordination of egoism to it, far beyond the point of absolute moral duty, should be one of the chief aims of education, both individual and collective . . . Nor can any pains taken be too great, to form the habit, and develop the desire, of being useful to others and to the world, by the practice, independently of reward and of every personal consideration, of positive virtue beyond the bounds of prescribed duty. No efforts should be spared to associate the pupil's self-respect, and his desire to respect others, with service rendered to humanity; when possible, collectively, but at all events, what is always possible, in the persons of its collective members.[28]

By placing minimal moral constraints upon everyone, and by encouraging but not requiring supererogation, Mill suggests, a society can create a climate where people will desire to live virtuous lives. The proper way to promote moral heroism is to create an environment conducive to altruism. This can be done primarily through education and the examples that are offered by virtuous individuals in the daily course of their lives. Given the right education and the right moral climate, people will desire to be altruistic; it becomes part of their personality and a key to their own self-respect.

Once again, moral sanctions are properly applied to those who harm others or refuse to honor their obligations; but this is completely consistent with moral minimalism. The importance of avoiding and preventing harm in Mill's overall system should not be underestimated, and I discussed Mill's Harm Principle in some detail in the previous chapter. For now, note that this emphasis on harm is what one would expect from moral minimalists who consider our moral obligations and duties to be primarily (i.e., most often and ordinarily) *negative* obligations and duties. Edwards does recognize some positive obligations and duties, and I will return to this point in the next chapter.

We are morally required not to harm others, not to interfere in their projects and goals, not to prevent them from exercising their essential interests, not to violate our contracts with them, and not to treat others in ways we would not wish to be treated. The extremist's conception of morality is essentially *positive*: We are morally required to comfort the afflicted, to donate much if not all of our resources above the subsistence level to those less fortunate than ourselves, to place the interests of others ahead of our own, to do as much for others as we possibly can through the most judicious use of our talents and resources, in a nutshell, to maximize goodness and minimize harm.

ix. MILL'S UTILITARIANISM AND *ON LIBERTY*

Mill considered *On Liberty* to be his magnum opus. His autobiography describes how he and his wife revised this work extensively and affirms his own belief in its paramount importance. Several pages in Mill's autobiography are devoted to the discussion of *On Liberty*, Mill's thought processes during its composition, and his belief that it was his work that would most likely stand the test of time. Mill did not suggest that *Utilitarianism* would stand the test of time. *Utilitarianism* was a 'little work' that received exactly one sentence in Mill's autobiography. Mill writes:

> The work of the years 1860 and 1861 consisted chiefly of two treatises, only one of which was intended for immediate publication. This was the 'Considerations on Representative Government' . . . The other treatise written at this time is the one which was published some years later [1869] under the title of 'The Subjection of Women' . . . Soon after this time I took from their repository a portion of the unpublished papers which I had written during the last years of our married life, and shaped them, with some additional matter, into the little work entitled 'Utilitarianism'; which was first published, in three parts, in successive numbers of Fraser's Magazine [1861], and afterwards reprinted in a volume.[29]

This last sentence, once again, is the sole reference to *Utilitarianism* in the *Autobiography*. Yet Mill's moral philosophy is often evaluated today through anthologized versions of *Utilitarianism* that are usually truncated forms of this little work. In his autobiography Mill says that *On Liberty* was constructed so carefully that:

> [T]here was not a single sentence of it that was not several times gone through by us together, turned over in many ways, and carefully weeded of any faults, either in thought or expression,

> that we detected in it . . . it far surpasses, as a mere specimen of composition, anything which had proceeded from me either before or since . . . The 'Liberty' is likely to survive longer than anything else I have written (with the possible exception of the 'Logic'), because [it is] a kind of philosophic text-book of a single truth . . . the importance, to man and society, of a large variety in types of character, and of giving full freedom to human nature to expand itself in innumerable and conflicting directions.[30]

This philosophical textbook would be irrelevant to a discussion of Mill's moral philosophy, if it did not contain any direct connection between Mill's ethical theory and his liberalism. But *On Liberty* does contain such a connection; in fact, the connection is quite explicit.

> I regard utility as the ultimate appeal on all ethical questions; but it must be utility in the largest sense, grounded on the permanent interests of man as a progressive being. Those interests, I contend, authorize the subjection of individual spontaneity to external control, only in respect to those actions of each, which concern the interest of other people. If any one does an act hurtful to others, there is a prima facie case for punishing him, by law, or, where legal penalties are not safely applicable, by general disapprobation. There are also many positive acts for the benefits of others that which he may rightfully be compelled to perform; such as, to give evidence in a court of justice; to bear his fair share in the common defence, or in any other joint work necessary to the interest of the society to which he enjoys protection; and to perform certain acts of individual beneficence, such as saving a fellow creature's life, or interposing to protect the defenseless against ill-usage, things which whenever it is obviously a man's duty to do, he may rightfully be made responsible to society for not doing. A person may cause evil to others not only because of his actions but by his inaction, and in either case he is justly accountable to them for the injury. The latter case, it is true, requires a much more cautious exercise of compulsion than the former. To make anyone answerable for doing evil to others, is the rule; to make him answerable for not preventing evil, is, comparatively speaking, the exception. Yet there are many cases clear enough and grave enough to justify that exception.[31]

Lyons noted that it would be wrong to interpret this passage as suggesting Mill thinks that we have obligations to act to positively benefit others. 'Positive acts for the benefit of others' in this passage does not mean 'acts for the *positive benefit* of others.'[32] Edwards suggests that this distinction is crucial because Mill only wishes to commit himself to positive obligations that would be necessary to meet '*minimal* essentials of well being.'[33] The examples that Mill provides in this passage all concern abstaining from harming others or preventing the harm of others. Our duties to help others are actually quite minimal.

At this point the received reading of Mill should be seen to be obviously wrong. Over and over in passage after passage Mill rejects both ethical extremism and the view that utilitarians as a whole are committed to ethical extremism. Thus, Mill simply cannot be read in any coherent fashion as a maximizing utilitarian. How, then, should he be read? What would a positive formulation of a non-maximizing utilitarianism look like?

x. *UTILITARIANISM* AND *A SYSTEM OF LOGIC*

The received view is that Mill wrote very little about ethical theory per se, and, of the little that he did write on ethical theory, the bulk of it can be found in *Utilitarianism*. This is particularly odd since the received view often accepts Mill's *A System of Logic* as his most important work. The incongruity of these two views is apparent when one realizes that Book VI of the latter work is entitled 'On the Logic of the Moral Sciences.' However, as Brown noted, by the early 1970s many Mill scholars had come to believe that the account of moral reasoning in *A System Of Logic* should govern our understanding of *Utilitarianism*.[34] Brown's view is, of course, consistent with Mill's telling us in his autobiography that *Utilitarianism* is a little work and that *A System of Logic* ranks with *On Liberty* as his most important works. The problem with relying on *Utilitarianism* as a full account of Mill's ethical views is that he seems to write in this work with two voices. At times he speaks in a very general tone that would apply to utilitarian theories as a whole, but at other times he makes very specific pronouncements that would be at odds with the utilitarianism of his father and Bentham. But Mill's speaking in general terms is often blown out of all proportion.

According to Fred Berger, the following passage is most often cited when commentators attempt to justify reading Mill as a maximizing act-utilitarian.[35] In Chapter II of *Utilitarianism* Mill writes:

> The creed which accepts as the foundation of morals, Utility, or the Greatest Happiness Principle, holds that actions are right in proportion as they tend to promote happiness, wrong as they tend to produce the reverse of happiness. By happiness is intended pleasure, and the absence of pain; by unhappiness, pain, and the privation of pleasure. To give a clear view of the moral standard set up by the theory, much more requires to be said; in particular, what things it includes in the ideas of pain and pleasure; and to what extent this is left an open question. But these supplementary explanations do not affect the theory of life on which this theory of morality is grounded – namely, that pleasure, and freedom from pain, are the only things desirable as ends; and that all desirable things (which are as numerous in the utilitarian as in any other scheme) are desirable either for the pleasure inherent in themselves, or as means to the promotion of pleasure and the prevention of pain.[36]

Of course, the main problem for reading this passage as the expression of a maximizing act-utilitarian Mill is that if Mill is suggesting that we should maximize utility, why does he not simply use this phrase? As M. S. J. Packe notes in his biography of Mill, he was certainly familiar with the word 'maximize,' since it was Bentham who coined and popularized its usage.[37] This problem becomes quite acute for the maximizing act-utilitarian reading, since its supporters must explain why Mill uses 'promote' (and, indeed, 'tends to promote') when he means 'maximize.' After all, in standard usage, these words have quite distinct meanings. The only example that I am aware of where 'promote' can mean something close to 'maximize' comes from chess. Chess players often say 'promote a pawn' as shorthand for 'promote a pawn to a queen,' and occasionally use the phrase 'under-promote' to indicate a promotion to a lesser piece. But there is nothing incorrect with the expression 'promote to a bishop.' In general, 'promote a pawn' means promote to any one of several pieces, not simply the one with the maximum value. But neither Mill's autobiography nor Packe's biography indicate that Mill was an occasional, let alone serious, chess player.

It should be clear that good exegesis will not involve interpreting words outside their normal meaning without some textual analysis or support, or at least some explanation for how some specific community uses its technical terms. Since supporters of the maximizing act-utilitarian reading, in my experience, never offer any textual analysis or support for their reading, or any evidence that the classical utilitarians have a specific technical meaning for 'promote,' why are they not guilty of a Humpty-Dumptyism? It takes just a few sentences – note my chess player example – to present a coherent account of when a specific community's use of the term 'promote' should be interpreted as 'maximize.' Of course, the phrase 'in proportion as they tend to promote' does not roll off the tongue easily for those who were educated in the latter half of the twentieth century. For this reason, Berger has examined the use of these words in the writings of Bentham and John Austin, two critically important influences on Mill's education. Berger writes:

> The important fact to focus on is that a particular act can have numerous and manifold consequences. Moreover, an act can have consequences for many persons over a range of time. Some of these consequences may be good for some people and bad for others, thus making some people happy and others unhappy. Furthermore, it may have both good and bad consequences for the same person. In such cases, it makes sense to say that the act tends to promote happiness if, on balance, it produces more happiness than unhappiness, that is, if it acts predominately in the direction of happiness. The greater the difference between the total of bad consequences, the greater is its tendency to produce good with, we might add that it also makes sense to say that an act has some tendency to good if it has any good consequences, though, of course, that need not be its predominant tendency . . . Bentham and Austin explicitly adopted such a meaning for 'tendency' in explicating their versions of utilitarianism . . . Mill's use of this concept in regard to the rules governing conduct turns out to be equivalent to that of Bentham and Austin.[38]

Thus, if Berger is correct, Mill's 'acts are right in proportion as they tend to promote happiness, wrong as they tend to promote the reverse' is best interpreted as something like 'acts are right if they are likely, on balance, to produce more happiness than unhappiness.' This reading, of course, does not support the minimalist interpretation. However, it does suggest that this passage does little to advance the maximizing act-utilitarian position. It says nothing to the issue of whether one right act is preferable to another, let alone whether one would be morally required to perform one right act over another. Also, it should be noted that Berger suggests that Mill uses 'this concept in regard to the rules governing conduct.' If Berger's analysis is correct, it counts heavily against the act-utilitarian reading of Mill.

A System of Logic is quite helpful in clarifying the ambiguities about rules one finds in *Utilitarianism*. To begin this discussion it will be helpful to note the distinction that Mill makes between an art and a science. Today if one were to discuss the art of bread baking, one's audience would immediately have visions of a fabulously well paid and famous French pastry chef producing unique delicacies at a trendy Manhattan bistro. But what Mill meant by the art of bread baking would be the process the folks who work at the Kern's Bakery on Chapman Highway in Knoxville Tennessee employ to make bread on a daily basis. Clearly some science is involved in baking bread; and at a very general level one would use principles of biology, chemistry, and physics to bake bread. But a recipe does not resemble a science textbook. Instead it is a list of imperatives: heat the oven to *x* degrees, mix *y* amounts of flour with *z* amounts of yeast, etc. Of course, a trained scientist could give an account based on the relevant scientific theories about why you heat the oven to *x* degrees, but this is not what the folks at the bakery require. What they require is instead a set of secondary rules that have been derived from the relevant sciences.

> The grounds, then, of every rule of art, are to be found in the theorems of science. An art, or a body of art, consists of the rules, together with as much of the speculative propositions as comprises the justification of those rules. The complete art of any matter, includes a selection of such a portion from the science, as is necessary to show on what conditions the effects, which the art aims at producing, depend. And art in general, consists of the truths of science, arranged in the most convenient order for practice, instead of the order which is most convenient for thought. Science groups and arranges its truths, so as to enable us to take in at one view as much as possible of the

> general order of the universe. Art . . . follows them only into such of their detailed consequences as have led to the formation of rules of conduct.[39]

Science consists of theorems that are arranged specifically to allow us to conceptualize the universe. An art, or body of art, exists primarily to provide rules of conduct that put the truths of science into practical use. To bake bread one does not need to engage in conceptualizing anything at all. One simply needs a recipe.

What should an art provide? Science can explain how it is possible to bake bread, but it cannot provide a reason for doing so. Science can explain how different varieties of bread are possible, but it cannot explain why one would be preferable to another.

> But though the reasoning that connects the end or purpose of every art with its means, belongs to the domain of Science, the definition of the end itself belongs to Art, and forms its peculiar province. Every art has one first principle, or general major premise not borrowed from science; that which enunciates the object aimed at, and affirms it to be a desirable object . . . Propositions of science assert a matter of fact; an existence, a coexistence, a succession, or a resemblance. The propositions now spoken of do not assert anything that is, but enjoin or recommend that something should be.[40]

Medicine as an art assumes that it is valuable to cure the sick. Agriculture as an art assumes that it is important to grow some plants rather than others, to grow some plants in conjunction with others, or perhaps not to grow some plants at all. Science tells us it is possible to increase the amount of grain grown per acre by third world farmers, but it would be up to an art to tell us whether we should do so.

One of the keys for understanding Mill's ethical theory is to get a clear conception of what Mill means by an art, and then to realize that for Mill morality is an art and not a science. In fact morality is a sub-art, a subset of what Mill calls the 'Art of Life.' Once we get clear on the difference between art and science we could form:

> a body of doctrine, which is properly called the Art of Life, in its three departments, Morality, Prudence or Policy, and Aesthetics;

> the Right, the Expedient, and the Beautiful or Noble, in human conduct and works. To this art, (which, in the main, is unfortunately still to be created) all other arts are subordinate; since its principles are those which must determine whether the special aim of any art is worthy and desirable, and what is its place in the scale of desirable things. Every art is thus a joint result of laws of nature disclosed by science, and of the general principles of what has been called Teleology, or the Doctrine of Ends.[41]

Morality, for Mill, is a sub-art and merely a piece of Mill's overall axiological picture. But recall that the key function of an art is to adapt our scientific understanding in a way that allows us to accomplish practical goals. Science tells us what we can do, not what we should do. Science tells us how to bake bread, but the art of bread making exists because human beings believe it is desirable to do so. If there is a Millian Art of Life, then there must be a purpose for this art. If there is a teleology, there must be a telos. Finally, it is possible to place the Principle of Utility in Mill's larger axiological scheme.

> Without attempting in this place to justify my opinion or even to define the kind of justification which it admits of, I merely declare my conviction, that the general principle to which all rules of practice ought to conform, and the test by which they should be tried, is that of conduciveness to the happiness of mankind, or rather all sentient beings: in other words, that the promotion of happiness is the ultimate principle of teleology.[42]

Mill does not mention maximizing happiness in this passage. He is merely looking for a principle to ground his axiology. He wants a criterion to which rules should be made to conform. This criterion would provide a test to determine if a rule is valid. One criterion for a rule's being moral is that it promotes happiness. Another would be that it passes the Brandt/Edwards teachability test. Another would be that it does not conflict with other moral rules. As the ACLU's Nadine Strossen could argue a sexual harassment regulation would be invalid if it did not promote happiness. But even if a regulation did promote happiness in the abstract, it would have to be evaluated in terms of its teachability and whether it would conflict with free speech considerations.

xi. THE PRINCIPLE OF UTILITY

Thus, promoting happiness is simply one criterion for an act to be moral. After a close reading of Mill's *Utilitarianism*, Brown found that Mill constructed multiple versions of the Principle of Utility that Mill considered equivalent. Happiness could be 'pleasure and freedom from pain' or 'an existence exempt as far as possible from pain, and as rich as possible in enjoyment, both in point of quantity and quality of happiness.' Happiness then could be 'desirable as an end,' the 'ultimate end of action,' 'good as an end,' 'in itself good,' or 'intrinsically good.'[43] Combining these two lists one could form ten possible formulations of the principle of utility. What Brown finds is that all of these formulations can be summarized to form the following core version of the principle of utility: 'Happiness is the only thing desirable as an end.'[44]

I will suggest later that this is more than a little misleading, but probably is sufficient for many applications. One clear defect in this formulation of the Principle of Utility is it omits the imperative element of Mill's morality, that is, as Edwards notes, it omits 'it is desirable to promote.'[45] As I have previously suggested, this principle is the first principle for all three parts of Mill's Art of Life. Moral acts, expedient acts, and aesthetic acts will all have the principle of utility as their first principle, and moral acts will promote happiness. But simply because an act promotes happiness, does not mean that it is morally obligatory, especially if the happiness is one's own. The minimalist aspect of Mill's utilitarianism allows Mill to suggest that performing acts that promote happiness is either prudentially or morally praiseworthy, but in only a limited number of cases are acts that promote happiness morally obligatory. Mill discusses moral obligation in detail in *Utilitarianism*.

> The idea of penal sanction, which is the essence of law, enters not only into the conception of justice, but into that of any kind of wrong. We do not call anything wrong, unless we mean that a person ought to be punished in some way or other for doing it; if not by law, by the opinion of his fellow creatures; if not by opinion, by the reproaches of his own conscience. This seems to be the real turning point of the distinction between morality and simple expediency. It is part of the notion of Duty in every one of its forms, that a person may rightfully be compelled to fulfill it. Duty is a thing which may be exacted from a person, as one

> exacts a debt. Unless we think that it may be exacted from him, we do not call it his duty. Reasons of prudence, or the interests of other people, may militate against exacting it; but the person himself, it is clearly understood, would not be entitled to complain. There are other things, on the contrary, which we wish people to do, which we like or admire them for doing, perhaps dislike or despise them for not doing, but yet admit that they are not bound to do; it is not a case of moral obligation; we do not blame them, that is, we do not think that they are proper objects of punishment.[46]

Mill clearly wanted the domain of moral duties to be limited. The above passage explains that there are cases of immoral acts, and that morality should be enforced, but 'immoral' is a much stronger word than 'inexpedient.' When a person behaves inexpediently he or she has acted in a manner that promotes personal disutility, or perhaps harms others in non-objectionable ways, but when a person acts immorally, he or she has promoted disutility for others in a way that deserves punishment, whether it be legal sanction, the condemnation of others, or their own personal feeling of guilt.

Mill, in his 1838 essay 'Bentham,' both compliments and criticizes Bentham's work. Recall that on Mill's account, Bentham was 'not a great philosopher, but a great reformer in philosophy.' Mill found much of Bentham's contribution to be entirely negative in showing the ambiguity and unclarity, if not outright error, of his opponents. Mill considered Bentham's primary positive contribution to be his methodology. Bentham introduced into morals and politics 'those habits of thought and modes of investigation' that make scientific inquiry possible.[47] Mill does not consider Bentham the inventor of the principle of utility. Mill actually found this principle in the philosophies of Socrates and Aristotle. Bentham's use of the principle of utility, however, does offer a keen insight that Mill considers invaluable as a contribution to axiological methodology.

> It is probable, however, that to the principle of utility we owe all that Bentham did; that it was necessary to him to find a first principle which he could receive as self-evident, and to which he could attach all his other doctrines as logical consequences: that to him systematic unity was an indispensable condition of his confidence in his own intellect . . . Whether Happiness be or not

> be the end to which morality should be referred – that it be referred to an *end* of some sort, and not left in the dominion of vague feeling or inexplicable conviction, that it be made a matter of reason and calculation, and not merely of sentiment, is essential to the very idea of moral philosophy; is, in fact, what renders argument or discussion on moral questions possible.[48]

Bentham's key contribution, Mill insists, is the principle that morality must be grounded in something. As we have seen earlier, Mill the empiricist and naturalist was more than distrustful of intuitionism. People's intuitions are often hopelessly flawed. One can meet people today who doubt the importance of the North winning the Civil War. Even the best of us recognize that our intuitions, at least upon occasion, fail us. As a mathematics professor of mine, Frank H. Beatrous, Jr., once put it 'that is why we prove things.' He joked 'I doubt my intuitions are correct one time in twenty.' If anything, the moral problems Mill wants to wrestle with are more counter-intuitive than pure mathematics. Without a ground to our axiology all we would have is our intuitions, and Mill finds this unacceptable. If we cannot reason and engage in ethical calculation, Mill suggests that moral philosophy and moral argumentation become impossible.

However, Mill also suggests that 'under proper explanation' he will accept Bentham's principle of utility, but must disagree 'that all right thinking on the details of morals depends on its express assertion.' Mill writes:

> We think utility, or happiness, much too complex and indefinite an end to be sought except through the medium of secondary ends, concerning which there may be, and often is, agreement among persons who differ in there ultimate standard; and about which there does in fact prevail a much greater unanimity among thinking persons . . . Those who adopt utility as a standard can seldom apply it truly except through the secondary principles; those who reject it, generally do no more than erect those secondary principles into first principles. It is when two or more of the secondary principles conflict, that a direct appeal to some first principle becomes necessary; and then commences the practical importance of the utilitarian controversy; which is, in other respects, a question of arrangement and logical subordin-

> ation rather than of practice; important principally in a purely scientific point of view, for the sake of the systematic unity and coherency of ethical philosophy.[49]

In almost all practical situations Mill would never appeal to the principle of utility. It would involve unnecessary and overly complex calculation. It may be that the calculation is too complex to complete. Mill suggested in *Utilitarianism* that it is necessary to apply secondary rules in all practical situations regardless of our moral theory. Even fundamentalist Christians who have faith in the literal truth and inerrancy of the Bible cannot stop to read the entirety of the Bible to find an applicable passage every time they must make a decision. This is why they study the Bible; one then knows where the relevant passage is. Similarly, utilitarians will not always be able to calculate; but it is not necessary to do so. We have thousands of years of human history to guide in the formation of our secondary principles. Secondary principles under normal circumstances will suffice. The principle of utility primarily provides a methodology to facilitate conflict resolution when secondary principles are at odds with each other.

The following kind of case illustrates this point: If we decrease the prosecution's burden of proof in rape cases, we could decrease the prevalence of rape; but more innocent defendants will be convicted and unjustly punished. Should this be done? There is no easy answer. Either decision ensures that innocent people will suffer. Without a first principle to apply there is no reasonable way to even formulate a procedure to resolve such conflicts.

The principle of utility gives us a methodology. We can examine the questions of morality through an empirisistic and naturalistic lens. We can ask how much rape victims suffer. We can ask how much innocent convicts suffer. We can try hypothetically to weigh the change in utility that the proposed legislation would produce and ask whether it is positive or negative. We may not be able in practice to answer these questions. As Aristotle noted long ago, ethics is not geometry. Ethics is much less precise, and we can adequately engage in ethical discussion only if we seek the amount of accuracy that is possible for the discipline.[50] The principle of utility makes Mill's ethics complete. We may not in practice be able to resolve a particular dilemma, but in theory we always can find a just resolution. Intuitionists may also claim that their ethics is complete. Perhaps for any case they have a clear intuition, but the ethical intuitionist lacks any procedure to rectify mistakes. Any of Mill's secondary principles is, in principle, capable of being proved wrong. They are testable in a way that the a priori moralist's intuitions are not. If adopting the Harm Principle actually could be shown to produce more harm than good in the long run Mill would be forced to reject it. Thus, the Principle of Utility offers a procedure that could show any of Mill's secondary principles false. But since Mill wants his ethics to be scientific this is to be expected. A debate between moral intuitionists is unenlightening. How exactly should one attempt to try to convince others that their moral intuitions are wrong? What procedure does one use? Utilitarians who disagree about secondary rules can appeal to the Principle of Utility.

xii. UTILITY AND CHARACTER FORMATION

Mill also wished to stress another failure in Bentham's system. Bentham completely ignores the formation of character and the importance of self-development in the formation of character. He ignores the importance of helping others to engage in the moral process.

> Morality consists of two parts. One of these is self-education; the training, by the human being himself, of his affections and will. That department is a blank in Bentham's system. The other and co-equal part, the regulation of his outward actions, must be altogether halting and imperfect without the first; for how can we judge in what manner many an action will affect even the worldly interests of ourselves and others, unless we take in, as part of the question, its influence on the regulation of our, or their, affections and desires? A moralist on Bentham's principles may get as far as this, that he ought not to slay, burn, or steal; but what will be his qualifications for regulating the nicer shade of human behavior, or for laying down even the greater moralities as to those facts in human life which tend to influence the depth of character quite independently of any influence on worldly circumstances – such, for instance, as the sexual relations, or those of family in general, or any other social and sympathetic connexions of any intimate kind? The moralities of these

> questions depend essentially on considerations which Bentham never so much as took into the account; and when he happened to be in the right, it was always, and necessarily, on wrong or in sufficient grounds.[51]

Alan Ryan has written that 'Mill's concern with self-development and moral progress is a strand in his philosophy to which almost everything else is subordinate.'[52] Precisely for this reason, Mill must distance himself from Bentham. Bentham never considers the long-term utility that is inherent in character formation. How could he? For Bentham, as I have noted, pushpin could be considered better than poetry! It is not necessary for my purposes to engage in a lengthy discussion of what Mill meant by higher and lower pleasures. It is enough to recognize that Mill believed that the long-term utility of any society is greatly enhanced by encouraging members of that society to reach their full potential. Perhaps the best way individuals can contribute to society is by becoming the best person they possibly can. As noted earlier, Mill was learning Greek philosophy as a child. The Greek acceptance of the importance of virtue was never questioned. One way of explaining the mental crisis was that the tension between Plato and Bentham could no longer be reconciled. He must modify Bentham to keep a heroic vision for Socrates. In the penultimate paragraph of *A System of Logic* Mill wrote:

> I do not mean to assert that the promotion of happiness should be itself the end of all actions, or even of all rules of action. It is the justification, and ought to be the controller, of all ends, but it is not itself the sole end. There are many virtuous actions, and even virtuous modes of action (though the cases are, I think, less frequent than is often supposed) by which happiness in the particular instance is sacrificed, more pain being produced than pleasure. But conduct of which this can be truly asserted, admits of justification only because it can be shown that on the whole more happiness will exist in the world, if feelings are cultivated which will make people, in certain cases, regardless of happiness. I fully admit that this is true: that the cultivation of an ideal nobleness of will and conduct, should be to individual human beings an end, to which the specific pursuit either of their own happiness or of that of others (except so far as included in that

> idea) should, in any case of conflict, give way. But I hold that the very question, what constitutes this elevation of character, is itself to be decided by a reference to happiness as the standard. The character itself should be, to the individual, a paramount end, simply because the existence of this ideal nobleness of character, or of a near approach to it, in any abundance, would go further than all things else towards making human life happy; both in the comparatively humble sense, of pleasure and freedom from pain, and in the higher meaning, of rendering life, not what it now is almost universally, puerile and insignificant – but such as human beings with highly developed faculties can care to have.[53]

Brown was thus wrong when he asserted that for Mill happiness is the only thing desirable as an end. Clearly there is a second primary principle, namely, develop a virtuous character. Often the most important contribution we can make to society is to develop our talents and our capacities for virtuous conduct. This is perhaps the primary reason that Mill must reject the Extremist's conception of morality. The Extremist is so focused in the here and now that the importance of the full development of one's own character is never considered. The Extremist does not appreciate the long-term benefits to my own character development and the resulting benefits to my own happiness and the happiness of others that might ensue from a decision to go to the movies. The Extremist suggests that I should visit the sick instead. But if I never go to the movies or engage in activities that enrich my personality, why would anyone wish for me to visit them? The Extremist is a prig and a bore. Having spent all of his or her life attempting to maximize utility, he or she ends up with little to contribute to it.

John Gray characterized Mill as an indirect utilitarian.[54] As in the paradox of hedonism, Mill thinks it will often be counterproductive to try to maximize utility. The sophisticated hedonist recognizes that short-term pains may lead to long-term pleasures. Similarly, the sophisticated utilitarian must think in terms of the long run. The greatest amount of utility will be produced by not pursuing it directly. By calling Mill an indirect utilitarian, Gray makes explicit a key feature of Mill's utilitarianism that any respectable Millian exegesis must include.

In discussing the inadequacy of virtue theory, James Rachels, who perhaps I have treated harshly in some of my written work, makes an observation as keen and insightful as his Millian exegesis is flawed. Virtue theory is flawed in that many commendable acts do not seem to have a corresponding virtue. However virtue theory should be part of a complete moral theory. A total theory is needed that both gives an account of right actions and also a related account of virtuous character that does justice to both. Rachels suggests this is possible:

> Our overall theory might begin by taking human welfare – or the welfare of all sentient creatures, for that matter – as the surpassingly important value. We might say that, from a moral point of view, we should want a society in which all people can live happy and satisfying lives. We could then go on to consider the question of what sorts of actions and social policies would contribute to this goal *and* the question of what qualities of character are needed to create and sustain individual lives. An inquiry into the nature of virtue could profitably be conducted from within the perspective that such a larger view would provide. Each would illuminate the other; and if each part of the overall theory had to be adjusted here and there to accommodate the other, so much the better for truth.[55]

This is a compelling, if brief, account of what an adequate virtue theory would look like. If Rachels had been discussing Mill, it would be a nice summary of what Mill wished to accomplish. Although this is not Rachels' intention, his summary meshes nicely with the overall axiology that I have ascribed to Mill in this chapter. Mill certainly begins by taking promoting the welfare of sentient beings as his first principle. Mill wants a society where people live satisfying lives. Mill certainly wants individuals to develop their natural gifts and capacities, to be capable of appreciating the higher pleasures. All of this is consistent with wanting people to live virtuous lives. Perhaps the key reason for adopting secondary principles as our primary guide to life is that these secondary principles can be adjusted to reconcile our desires for human happiness with our desires for human progress and moral development.

This distinction I am drawing between Bentham and Mill is hardly original. It is a commonplace in the literature to distinguish

Bentham's hedonistic utilitarianism from Mill's eudaimonistic utilitarianism. But having made this distinction, it is often dropped too quickly. A hedonist may well justify actions based on maximizing hedons. A eudaimonist will need a richer set of criteria. I will return to this point in the next chapter.

xiii. THE CHOICE OF HERCULES

In the part of the autobiography where he discusses the moral influences of his early youth, Mill emphasizes how strongly he was affected by the character of Socrates, how Socrates stood in his mind as a 'model of ideal excellence,' and how strong were his father's exhortations of the Socratic virtues. He also remembered how his father impressed upon him the lesson of the 'Choice of Hercules.'[56]

Early in his adulthood, Hercules considered the road he should follow in life. While he pondered this question two women approached him. The first, named Happiness (her enemies called her Vice), suggested to Hercules that he should follow her. He would live a life without hardships of any kind. He would experience all the pleasures of life without labors of any kind. The second, named Virtue, suggested that without labor none of the goods that are worth having would be available. She told Hercules that to be honored by others one must be honorable. It takes sacrifice to accomplish the goals that make life worth living.

Hercules chose to follow virtue. James Mill stressed the importance of this choice to his son. Any account of either Mill's utilitarianism should be able to explain why this is so. I believe that the account of John Stuart Mill's utilitarianism offered in this chapter does so more than adequately. Hercules recognized that the pleasures of a life of virtue are qualitatively superior to the pleasures of a life of vice. Mill rejected Bentham's utilitarianism partly because Bentham was unable to recognize this.

Edwards' reading of Mill is an adequate account of Mill's utilitarianism. Edwards tells us what Mill believed. My only addition to Edwards is to ask: why? The answer is that Mill wished to adopt an axiology that is not grounded in intuitions. He wanted to use the principle of utility as a foundation of an axiology that allows human beings the largest possible capacity for self-development and character formation. He wanted a utilitarianism that is fully consistent with human progress and moral development. The received view prevents us from seeing why human freedom is important to Mill, and the relationship between freedom and self-development, and the formation of character. Edwards' characterization of Mill allows us to see this and more. Read as a minimalist utilitarian, Mill can be consistently viewed both as a consequentialist, and as a supporter of rights.

CHAPTER 5

MILL AND HUMAN RIGHTS

i. RACIAL AND GENDER JUSTICE

I think any serious assessment of Mill's morals and politics must begin with the important civil rights struggles of our era, namely, the struggles for racial and gender justice. The questions are: How comprehensive is a utilitarian theory of rights? Can it protect important rights of individuals and minority groups yet still be faithful to democratic ideals and the common good? How good is a utilitarian theory of rights when compared to its rivals? The usual answer is that Mill and utilitarianism fail, and in any case Kant and Kantianism are clearly superior. Writing on this issue Vincent Barry says:

> But do individuals have moral rights? Are they merely by virtue of being human beings, entitled to act in certain ways and expect others to act in certain ways human rights? Without hesitation, Kant answered in the affirmative. He believed that all persons have unique and equal worth as human beings, which is theirs independently of the decisions or acts of anyone else. As a result, they are entitled – that is, have a moral right – to be treated with dignity and respect as free and equal persons; and all of us have a duty to so treat others.[1]

Barry's view is that utilitarians are somehow unable to suggest that, say, blacks and women are entitled to the same rights as white men. Barry writes:

> Utilitarianism, in effect, treats all such 'entitlements' as subordinate to the general good. Thus individuals are 'entitled' to act in

> a certain way and entitled to have others allow or even aid them to so act only insofar as the greatest good is effected. The assertion of moral rights, therefore, decisively sets all nonconsequentialists, and Kant in particular, apart from utilitarians.[2]

Students of history, however, will find these results surprising. As a matter of historical fact utilitarians such as Bentham and the Mills were considered radicals on these issues. The Utilitarian Radicals were extreme egalitarians. They held the extreme views about extending the franchise to then disenfranchised groups. This is all well known. As a matter of historical fact John Stuart Mill's views on race and gender are still progressive (perhaps even radical) today, and no one but the vilest of bigots would accept Kant's. Eventually, I wish to show that what these men actually believed is not simply an accident of history, and that there are important moral and philosophical lessons to be learned. But to accomplish this I must first examine what Immanuel Kant and John Stuart Mill actually believed. I will begin with Kant.

ii. KANT ON RACE

Kant's *Observations on the Feeling of the Beautiful and Sublime* is at its best a tribute to ethnic stereotyping. Page after page finds Kant waxing poetic on the purported national character of various Europeans; the French are like this, the Spanish are like that, the English have these characteristics, the Italians have those, and unsurprisingly the Germans are the best at combining the beautiful and the sublime. Since the Europeans all have various positive and negative attributes, most of Kant's observations are harmless (perhaps silly) fun. He even allows in a footnote that among the Europeans there are exceptions to his various rules. However when he turns to Africa he has this to say:

> The Negroes of Africa have by nature no feeling that rises above the trifling. Mr. Hume challenges anyone to cite a single example in which a Negro has shown talents, and asserts that among the hundreds of thousands of blacks who are transported elsewhere from their countries, although many of them have even been set free, still not a single one was ever found who presented anything great in art or science or any other praiseworthy quality,

> even though among the whites some continuously rise aloft from the lowest rabble, and through superior effort earn respect in the world. So fundamental is the difference between these two races of man, and it appears to be as great in regard to mental capacities as in color. The religion of fetishes so widespread among them is perhaps a sort of idolatry that sinks as deeply into the trifling as appears to be possible to human nature. A bird feather, a cow's horn, a conch shell, or any other common object, as soon as it becomes consecrated by a few words, is an object of veneration and of invocation in swearing oaths. The blacks are very vain but in the Negro's way, and so talkative that they must be driven apart from each other with thrashing.[3]

Kant's views on race are almost self-explanatory. A Kantian apologist might wish to argue that Kant is simply making cultural observations. But his ringing endorsement of David Hume most certainly answers the question whether Kant finds black inferiority to be cultural or biological. In his essay 'Of National Characters' (certainly Kant's source for the above) Hume finds 'Negroes to be naturally inferior to whites.' Noting major differences between Europeans and Africans Hume writes: 'Such a uniform and constant difference could not happen, in so many countries and ages, if nature had not made an original distinction between these breeds of men.' Hume goes on to dismiss a report of an educated Black Jamaican since it is likely that he is 'admired for slender accomplishments, like a parrot who speaks a few words plainly.'[4]

iii. RACIAL BLINDNESS

There are at least three ways of explaining the Kantian/Humean blindness about race. A first uncharitable reading suggests that these authors are simply guilty of selective amnesia. Evidence that would refute their racial classifications is simply downplayed or ignored. Assuming their own cultural superiority, they ethnocentrically accept any differences between European and African cultures as proof of African primitivism without ever attempting to examine them from an African point of view. A multicultural attempt to see Africa through African eyes might well have led to a greater respect for divergent social constructions. There is probably some truth to this view.

A second uncharitable reading suggests that white racism was a result of the black slave trade. The cruelty inflicted upon blacks during slavery cannot be underestimated. The natural reaction is revulsion for the slavers, and pity for their victims, unless one can somehow be convinced that blacks are so fundamentally different that normal standards of inhumanity do not apply to them. Slavery can only be accepted in a state of psychological denial. Once again, this explanation probably contains an element of truth.

A third more charitable explanation is offered by Dinesh D'Souza. In *The End of Racism* he argues that the eighteenth-century Europeans were attempting with the limited tools available to them to explain the civilization gap between Europe and Africa. Europe had universities where philosophical and theological texts dating back thousands of years were studied. Africa still had pre-literate societies. Europeans had calculus and analytic geometry. The Pythagoreans of ancient Greece knew about the irrationality of the square root of two. Some African societies had no numbers above two. There was a civilization gap to be explained, and the intellectuals of the modern era required an explanation with some scientific plausibility.[5]

Hume and Kant lived in the era before Darwin. A belief in the creationist account found in the Bible was almost universal. Bishop Usher's view that the earth was created in 4004 B.C. was by 1650 widely accepted. If humans were created by God less than 6000 years previously, a civilization gap of several thousand years seems enormous. Europeans also had a long history of accepting the biological origin of noble and base characteristics. For centuries, this was the justification for a largely hereditary aristocracy. When one combines these two views, a biological explanation for racial differences is plausible. By analogy, if one runner beats another runner in a 6000 meter race by 3000 meters, we would probably believe the first runner to be much more naturally gifted. (Of course, if the race were 200,000 meters, a difference of 3000 meters would suggest a close race.)

Today a biological explanation of this sort seems implausible; almost nobody will accept a 6000-year-old earth, and a hereditary ruling class. Darwinian evolution and meritocracy have replaced Usher's theology and aristocracy. But we should not judge eighteenth-century ethnocentrists ethnocentrically. Hume and Kant should be judged in relation to the tools available to them. But we should not be unaware of the mistakes they made, and why they made them. In particular, I think modern Kantians should not simply ignore his racism. Later in this chapter, I will discuss why.

iv. MILL ON RACE

One can contrast Kant's racism with Mill's views on the racial issues of his era. Two stand out. The first is Mill's support for the North in the American Civil war. The fact that Mill supported the North in the Civil War is relatively well known and not terribly surprising. What is generally not known is how extreme his support was and how unpopular this view was even in English liberal circles. Much of England's economy depended on the cotton trade with the south. As Mill writes in his autobiography 'It was not generally believed in England, for the first year or two of the war, that the quarrel was one of slavery. There were men of high principle and unquestionable liberality of opinion, who thought it a dispute about tariffs.'[6] Thus, with no high principle involved the Northern naval embargo of the South was considered an illegitimate abridgement on English free trade. In what is usually considered the definitive biography of Mill, *The Life of John Stuart Mill*, Michael St. John Packe writes about Mill's understanding of the war:

> For Mill, who had studied its approach for years it was a clear-cut issue. The North's was 'the good cause.' John Brown was a 'true hero.' The South had launched 'an aggressive enterprise of the slave-owners to extend the territory of slavery'; their success would be 'a victory of the powers of evil'.[7]

If Mill's views seem radical to us today, James Loewen claims it is because of the poverty of high school history textbooks. In *Lies My Teacher Told Me* Loewen argues persuasively that the history of the Civil War that most Americans have been taught is an unadulterated pro-confederacy white washing.[8] In Loewen's view, as in Mill's, slavery was an evil institution, and the war was about slavery. The good guys beat the bad guys: end of story! But according to Loewen textbook publishers are so afraid of offending white southerners that the Confederacy can only be discussed in the most respectful terms. So, the myth of a noble South lives on. How else can one explain the reluctance of Republican presidential candidates to condemn in the mildest terms the Confederate flag? If Mill and Loewen are right – and I suspect they are – modern American supporters of the confederacy should be considered on a par with modern German supporters of National Socialism. If all right-thinking individuals now renounce the Southern slave trade as racist and inhuman, why treat the Confederacy so gingerly?

The second clear indication of the strength of Mill's racial commitment is the support he gave to the controversial John Brown. A closer examination of the abolitionist martyr Brown proves illuminating. Mill described John Brown as a hero; in his autobiography he writes: 'The saying of this true hero, after his capture, that he was worth more for hanging than any other purpose, reminds one, by its combination of wit, wisdom, and self-devotion, of Sir Thomas More.'[9]

A comparison to More should not be taken lightly. He is a major figure in English history, and widely admired today almost five hundred years after his death. He was a prolific author whose best-known work, *Utopia*, is still influential. He coined the term 'utopia' which can be considered an example of his irony and wit; as Jenny Mezciems notes the Latin 'utopia' 'fuses together two Greek prefixes . . . "eutopia" would mean "good place" and "outopia" would mean "no place." '[10] Thus a utopian society is both 'happy' and 'nowhere.' He was executed in 1535 for refusing to acknowledge Henry VIII as Supreme Head of the English Church after Henry married his second wife, Anne Boleyn, in 1533 and was excommunicated for adultery. Numerous authors have compared More's martyrdom, irony, character, and intellect to that of Socrates.[11] His legend is still celebrated in our era. He was canonized as a Saint in 1935. His martyrdom was further chronicled in Richard Bolt's popular 1960 play 'A Man for All Seasons.' The 1966 film based on this play won six Oscars including best picture, best director, and best actor. More literally was a man for all seasons. When Mill compares Brown to More it should be considered high praise indeed. Mill hoped that eventually the entire North would come to accept the rightness of 'the noble body of Abolitionists' and 'the voluntary martyr' John Brown.

In contrast with Mill's praise, Loewen notes that the most popular high school history textbooks describe Brown as a murderer, a lunatic, or both. But this was certainly not the view of Brown in the North when he was hanged or during the war. Frederick Douglas called Brown 'one of the greatest heroes known to American fame.' Harriet Tubman wished to join Brown at Harper's Ferry but was prevented by illness. On the day of his execution Black-owned businesses across the North shut their doors in mourning.[12] Northern troops marched into battle singing 'John Brown's Body.' A sample lyric of this marching song is: 'John Brown's body lies a-mouldering in his grave: His soul is marching on!' If this pattern seems familiar it is because the tune of 'John Brown's Body' was so popular it later became the basis of the well-known 'Battle Hymn of the Republic.'[13] As for Brown's purported lunacy, Loewen writes: 'No black person who met John Brown thought him crazy.' Henry David Thoreau eulogized Brown comparing him to Jesus of Nazareth and suggested similarities in their martyrdom at the hands of the state.[14] Thoreau spoke: 'Some eighteen hundred years ago Christ was crucified; This morning, perchance Captain Brown was hung . . . He is not Old Brown any longer; he is an angel of light.'[15]

Of course, this is hardly an uncontroversial way to describe a clearly controversial figure. Ken Chowder has called Brown the 'father of American terrorism.' In an article in *American Heritage* magazine he suggests that Brown had strengths and weaknesses that make him an oddly compelling figure to this day.

> He gets compared to anarchists, leftist revolutionaries and right-wing extremists. The spinning of John Brown, in short, is still going strong. But what does that make *him*? This much at least, is certain: John Brown is a vital presence for all sorts of people today . . . on the verge of his two hundredth birthday [May 9, 2000] John Brown is oddly present. Perhaps there is one compelling reason for his revival in this new millennium: Perhaps the violent, excessive, morally torn society John Brown represents so aptly was not just his own antebellum America but this land, now.'[16]

Overall, Chowder offers a balanced view of Brown. Brown was an important player, perhaps the most important, in the fight to end American slavery. But many of his actions, for example the Pottawatomie massacre, give evidence of a fanatical belief in the rightness of his goals, and the willingness to use almost any means to accomplish them. Perhaps the best way to describe Brown is, paradoxically enough, as both a terrorist and a hero. Atrocities were committed by both sides in the events that immediately preceded the war. By the time of the Pottawatomie massacre these events had escalated to obscene proportions.[17]

Additionally, Bentham and James Mill were leading abolitionists who helped end England's involvement in slavery. Mill also was a leader in the call for the prosecution of the Governor of Jamaica for his treatment of Black protestors in Jamaica in 1866.

v. KANT AND WOMEN

Kant's views on women in the *Observations* are hardly more inspiring, but do require some textual exegesis. Kant wishes to distinguish between two modes of thought: the beautiful and the sublime. The beautiful is the social, amusing, friendly and good-hearted nature of our existence. This provides our ability to feel compassion and connect socially with others. The beautiful is that which makes one a good companion. It facilitates our appreciation of comedy. It is the quality that makes one popular and lovable. The sublime, on the other hand, is the rational, moral, respectful, and noble nature of our being. This provides our ability to make considered judgments and rational analysis. It is the quality that makes one vital and esteemed. Obviously, it is best to have some blend of both qualities. A deficiency of the sublime would make one trivial and insignificant. A deficiency of the beautiful would make one abstruse and a bore.

> Understanding is sublime, wit is beautiful. Courage is sublime and great, artfullness is little but beautiful . . . Veracity and honesty are simple and noble; jest and pleasant flattery are delicate and beautiful. Graciousness is the beauty of virtue. Unselfish zeal to serve is noble; refinement (*politesse*) and courtesy are beautiful. Sublime attributes stimulate esteem, but beautiful ones, love. People in whom especially the feeling for the beautiful rises seek their sincere, steadfast, and earnest friends only in need, but choose jesting, agreeable, and courteous companions for company. There is many a person whom one esteems much too highly to be able to love him. He inspires admiration, but is too far above us for us to dare approach him with the familiarity of love.[18]

According to Kant, woman's nature more than tends toward the beautiful. Even as children, women like to be dressed up. They take particular pleasure in being 'adorned.' They 'love pleasantry' and enjoy trivialities particularly when they are humorous.[19] Women have a beautiful understanding, but lack a deep one. A woman who studies Greek or physics 'might as well have a beard.' The philosophy of 'women is not to reason but to sense.' Since Kantian moral agency is so dependent on the sublime, those that are lacking in it can hardly be taken seriously.

> The virtue of a woman is a *beautiful virtue*. That of the male sex should be a *noble virtue*. Women will avoid the wicked not because it is unright, but because it is ugly; and virtuous actions mean to them such as are morally beautiful. Nothing of duty, nothing of compulsion, nothing of obligation! Woman is intolerant of all commands and all morose constraint. They do something only because it pleases them, and the art consists in making only that please them which is good. I hardly believe that the fair sex is capable of principles . . .[20]

To understand how the above is such a serious condemnation of women it is necessary to familiarize ourselves with a bit of the details of Kant's moral philosophy. If one starts with Hume's Fork it is hard to know what to make of moral claims, say, 'All acts of polygamy are wrong.' Since the predicate term is not included in the subject term, it is clearly not an analytic a priori proposition. But categorical claims of this nature, such as 'all events have a cause, or 'all acts of polygamy are wrong,' cannot by Kant's analysis as discussed in Chapter 1 be synthetic a posteriori, so if moral claims makes sense they must be synthetic a priori claims derived from the supreme principle of morality that Kant called 'the categorical imperative.' Since women lack principles it is hard to see how they can be moral. Now one might be tempted to say that Kant might be claiming that women are inclined to be moral. But in an important distinction that Kant makes in his work *Groundwork of the Metaphysic of Morals* he makes an important distinction between actions done 'from duty' and acts done 'in accordance with duty.' Kant writes:

> To help others when one can is a duty, and besides this there are many spirits of so sympathetic a temper that, without any further

> motive of vanity or self-interest they find an inner pleasure in spreading happiness around them and can take delight of others as their own work. Yet I maintain that in such a case, however right and however amiable it may be, has still *no genuine moral worth*. It stands on the same footing as other inclinations . . . for its maxim lacks moral content, namely, the performance of such actions, not from inclination, but *from duty*.[21]

It is a matter of some scholarly dispute as to how strongly to take this, but even on a fairly charitable reading as given by H.J. Patton in his 'Analysis of the Argument' from this edition of the *Groundwork* puts it: 'It is the motive of duty, not the motive of action, that gives moral worth to an action.'[22] Thus, if Kant is correct, women are clearly not moral agents.

As I will argue in more detail later, the distinction between the beautiful and the sublime makes it difficult to take women, as well as other marginalized groups, seriously as moral agents. Moral agents are rational and act from duty. But the first line of defense for the Kantian is to suggest that the view of women offered in the *Observations* is not characteristic of Kant's moral thought. Writing on this issue, feminist Natalie Alexander has examined the imagery and allusions to women in Kant's work. This includes the entire Kantian corpus, and Alexander claims that she paid careful attention to Kant's later works including the *Critiques*. She suggests that Kant's views about women's actual nature exhibit an incoherency about the nature of women. According to Alexander, on Kant's view, women do not share the same relationship with morality or rational agency that men do. Women are not rational agents but 'sublime objects.' Women are thus things for sublime agents to objectify. This Kantian image of women should be contrasted with a Kantian view of men: Men are autonomous subjects with their own 'rational agency.' She concludes:

> I argue that the incoherence of Kant's views of women becomes clear. More finely crafted as nature's tools, women have a different relation to moral law, to rational agency than men do. In Kant's schema of relation between the sexes, the woman must make of herself the object of respect; woman herself is primarily a representation for men . . . the feminine image only serves, for Kant, to represent the masculine subject's own rational agency.

> There is no real place in Kant's moral theorizing for women as subjects, either as agents of their own desires or as rational moral agents.[23]

vi. MILL AND FEMINIST ACTIVISM

Mill's credentials as a feminist are well known and I will not repeat them here. He was the only major philosopher prior to the twentieth century who can reasonably be called a feminist. One incident in Mill's life is not as well known and is worth repeating. During Mill's lifetime poverty and a lack of information concerning birth control made infanticide common. When Mill was seventeen he came across an abandoned dead infant in a park. Mill's reaction was not to blame working class women, but to consider alternatives. He consulted with the liberal Malthusian, Francis Place. Place convinced Mill that what was needed was for working class women to have better access to family planning information. Place was wealthy, and thus had the time and money to write and publish a book on population control. He also wrote and published a shorter and less abstruse pamphlet, one that could be practically applied by the working class. Armed with these pamphlets, Mill and a friend distributed them in locations where working class women would be sure to find them. Mill and his friend were eventually arrested and jailed until a magistrate could be found. Packe reports that there are conflicting accounts of what happened next, but the 'most likely scenario' is that they were jailed for a day or two on the charge of 'attempting to corrupt the purity of English womanhood.'[24]

vii. THE HISTORICAL MILL AND THE HISTORICAL KANT

Mill thought a white abolitionist's decision to fight and die for the freedom of blacks heroic; Kant believed that blacks should be thrashed when they talk too much. Mill was a committed feminist who was actually arrested and apparently jailed for feminist activism; Kant believed women to be less than rational. And yet Mill is required to meet counter-factuals contrary to his beliefs, while Kant's actual beliefs are ignored. Why is this important? Because there can be no sensible discussion of a philosopher's political and ethical views without some examination of his or her metaphysics. To address the question 'How should people live?' one must first answer the question 'What are people like?' In addition, rights talk can be very vague. As I suggested earlier I am troubled by Kant's racism for more than historical reasons. To this I now turn my attention.

The second line of defense for Kantian apologists is to suggest that while racism and sexism were prevalent in his era, Kant's views are neither extreme nor indicative of some core moral problem for his theory. As D'Sousza has shown these views were commonplace, and after all, Kant is certainly no worse than many other significant philosophical figures such as, previously noted, David Hume. However, there is a troubling issue or two here, and these issues can only fruitfully be examined after a consideration of Kant's views on animals.

viii. KANT AND ANIMALS

In a lecture on animals, recorded by his student, Georg Collins, Kant reportedly said:

> But since all animals exist only as means, and not for their own sakes, in that they have no self-consciousness, whereas man is the end, such that I can no longer ask: Why does he exist?, as can be done with animals; our duties towards them are indirect duties to humanity.[25]

Clearly animals have no rights, and our duties to them are non-existent. Our duties to animals are simply instrumental; to the extent that treating animals badly would prevent our cultivating our duty to humans, treating animals cruelly is wrong. We should avoid treating animals badly, since we should develop our capacities to 'promote the cause of humanity.' Thus, we should avoid treating animals in ways that would undermine this goal. Collins' notes continue:

> So if a man has his dog shot, because it can no longer earn a living for him, he is by no means in breach of any duty to the dog, since the latter is incapable of judgment, but he thereby damages the kindly and humane qualities in himself, which he ought to exercise in virtue of his duties to mankind.[26]

Kant goes on to note that engaging in cruelty to animals could harm our capacity for compassion, and might lead to losing this capacity even for humans. He notes an example, in England it is commonly believed that butchers, doctors, and surgeons are so 'inured to death' that they are incapable of making judgments about their fellow beings and are thus kept off of juries. There is nothing uniquely Kantian about the view that we should not kill animals for no or trivial reasons. But Kant suggests that it is natural for us to respect life in all its forms, and that we should not kill an animal for no reason. We should avoid this, since this tendency might subsequently be 'transferred to man.'[27] But Kant does suggest that cruelty to animals is justified if one has a good reason.

> So when anatomists take living animals to experiment on, that is certain cruelty, though there it is employed for a good purpose; because animals are regarded as man's instruments . . .[28]

But there are two problems with this: The least troubling of the two is that much of Kant's empirical reasoning is suspicious. We no longer prevent butchers, doctors, and surgeons from serving on juries. Why is this the case? We reject Kant's notion that these professions disqualify people from making important moral judgments. In a capital case, as in any other, the defense attorneys have an obligation to remove from the jury those individuals whom they find prejudicial to their client. In capital cases the issues become quite intense. But it would be rare for an attorney to strike a juror for simply being a butcher. Butchers, qua butchering, are not moral brutes. No attorney would assume this, and no attorney would remove a butcher from a jury panel without some other relevant social data. Similarly, I am aware of no data that supports the general idea. Many vivisectionists are committed humanists; conversely, Hitler loved his dogs. Dr. Robert Sharpe has argued in his extremely thorough book *The Cruel Deception* that *all* animal experimentation is morally wrong. But nowhere in his book does he suggest that vivisectionists eventually turn to human victims, or that experimenting on animals predisposes one toward human cruelty. Peter Singer has argued that this idea is simply absurd; Singer suggests no relationship between a willingness to kill *humans* in one situation and another. He has written:

> There is, anyway, little historical evidence to suggest that a permissive attitude towards the killing of one category of human beings leads to a breakdown of restrictions against killing other humans. Ancient Greeks regularly killed or exposed infants, but appear to have been at least as scrupulous about taking the lives of their fellow-citizens as medieval Christians or modern Americans. In traditional Eskimo societies it was the custom for a man to kill his elderly parents, but the murder of a normal healthy adult was almost unheard of. I mention these practices not to suggest that they should be imitated, but only to indicate that lines can be drawn at places different from where we now draw them. If these societies could separate human beings into different categories without transferring their attitudes from one group to another, we with our more sophisticated legal systems and greater medical knowledge should be able to do the same.[29]

This argument is reinforced by the current American political scene, for example, advocates of the death penalty often oppose euthanasia. Sharpe has argued, moreover, that Kant's suggestion that anatomists' dissection of animals is 'employed for a good purpose' is nonsense. According to Sharpe, medical science was delayed almost 1400 years due to the false generalizations of vivisectionists. Animals and humans differ in important ways, and much of the information provided by animal anatomists was wrong. In any case, reliance on ancient Greek observations, such as those by Galen, was clearly wrong. Sharpe writes:

> Galen's dogmatic style, together with the Church's reluctance to allow dissection of human cadavers, meant that his errors became enshrined in medical teaching for nearly 14 centuries. Right up until the time of Vesalius, everything relating to anatomy, physiology and disease was referred back to Galen as a final authority from whom there could be no appeal. Few had the courage or the desire to embark on fresh clinical observations.[30]

Kant's era should be noted as the time when a dogmatic acceptance of antiquity (Galen's medical 'science') and religious prohibition against human dissection was being rejected. Thus, if Sharpe is correct, religious and moral arguments against human dissection were the major impediment to advancing medical science. Kant and other proponents of human 'sacredness' were clearly on the wrong side of history. Kant's examples do not work, but as I will argue in a few pages, this is typical of his real world arguments.

ix. KANT AND THE CAPACITY FOR RATIONALITY

More importantly, Kant is clear that animals are means – not ends-in-themselves. Since animals lack sufficient capacity to reason, they are not part of the Kingdom of Ends. Clearly, one key to Kant's morality is rationality. If you are capable of having the insight to recognize the moral law, you are in the Kingdom of Ends; else, you are out. Of course, many sociopaths have the capacity to reason, and some of them can reason quite well. Sociopaths lack some other capacity that allows one to act from duty. Perhaps fear of prison prevents some sociopaths from engaging in a life of crime. But to be a moral agent, in Kant's view, it is not enough to merely live in accordance with morality. Kant has suggested that the moral life is abstract and complicated; at least to the extent that acting on hypothetical and categorical imperatives requires abstract and complicated thought. In his famous distinction, Kant suggests that to live morally is to act from duty, not merely in accordance with duty. Thus, critically, it is not enough to simply have a functioning alternative moral code that allows one to act morally serendipitously; acting morally requires one to act from duty, to have a good will. The Kingdom of Ends is co-extensive with those beings capable of moral judgments. Beings incapable of acting rationally, from duty, and according to the categorical imperative are not ends-in-themselves.

But there are many other problems with rationality as the criterion for moral agency. First, what if this excludes many sentient creatures including marginal humans? What if it excludes most humans? What if virtually no creatures meet Kant's standards of rationality? This final suggestion is less absurd than most readings of Kant allow. Kantians invariably present 'rationality' in vague enough terms that it does not cause intuitive concerns. But I believe that a reader familiar with the twentieth century debates about I.Q. and intelligence should find a reliance on rationality a troubling basis for according humans, let alone other sentient creatures, rights. The issue of intelligence and moral behavior peaked in 1994 with the publication of Richard Herrnstein and Charles Murray's

The Bell Curve. This book argues that a whole host of social events, as diverse as marriage stability, job stability, income, education completed, criminal behavior, and other social indicators of well being, could be traced to native intelligence as measured by standard I.Q. tests. Much of the furor over this book revolved around the assertion that racial groups differ in native intelligence, but this was hardly an original contribution of Herrnstein and Murray. Psychometricians have been making this claim for decades. For example, the introductory paragraph to Arthur Jensen's 1972 book reads:

> '*Educability and Group Differences* deals with the fact that various subpopulations (social classes and ethnic groups) in the United States and elsewhere show marked differences in the distributions of those mental abilities most importantly related to educability and its occupational and socioeconomic correlates . . . My review of this evidence, with its impressive consistency, does, I believe, cast serious doubt on the currently popular explanations in terms of environment.'[31]

The most radical responses to these claims are to suggest that intelligence and other achievement tests are the products of a hopelessly elitist or racist ideology, or that they are too limited to be of any practical value, or to deny any innate differences in groups at all.[32] However, since intelligence tests have some predictive validity, I take these approaches simply to be avoiding hard and uncomfortable questions. John H. McWhorter's cleverly titled 2000 work *Losing the Race* is a recent discussion about the predictive validity of SAT scores and their purported racial bias. Although he thinks that ultimately this is a cultural problem, his third chapter documents that it is quite real. According to economist Walter Williams:

> If I believed in conspiracies, I'd see attempts to banish the SAT as a college admission tool as part of the education establishment's ongoing efforts to keep parents, students and the taxpaying public in the dark about the fraudulent quality of primary and secondary education.[33]

As to the supposed racism in this work Thomas Sowell noted:

> '*The Bell Curve* is a very sober, very thorough, and very honest book – on a subject where sobriety, thoroughness, and honesty are only likely to provoke cries of outrage.[34]

As Christina Hoff has noted:

> The trouble is that not all human beings are rational. Mentally retarded or severely brain-damaged human beings are sometimes much less intelligent than lower primates that have been successfully taught to employ primitive languages and make simple, logical inferences beyond the capacity of the normal three-year-old. The view that rationality is the qualifying condition for moral status has the awkward consequence of leaving unexplained our perceived obligations to non-rational humanity.[35]

Second, how rational is enough? Why should we declare some beings to be perfectly rational, and decide those that fall beneath this standard to be excluded from moral agency? The civil-war era feminist and abolitionist Sojourner Truth had this to say:

> They talk about this thing in the head; what do they call it? ['Intellect' whispered someone near by.] That's it. What's that got to do with women's rights or Negroes' rights? If my cup won't hold but a pint and yours holds a quart, wouldn't you be mean not to let me have my little half-measure full?[36]

The idea that all human beings are equally rational is either tautologous or absurd. If one is simply defining human beings as 'rational animals,' as Aristotle did, then certainly all human beings are rational. But then the exclusion of animals from the Kingdom of Ends is completely arbitrary. Hoff has called the idea that all and only humans are rights holders the 'humanist principle.' She writes:

> Without further argument the humanist principle is arbitrary. What must be adduced is an acceptable criterion for awarding special rights. But when we proffer a criterion based, say, on the capacity to reason or suffer, it is clearly inadequate either because it is satisfied by some but not all members of the species *Homo sapiens*, or because it is satisfied by them all – and many other animals as well.[37]

But, on the other hand if Kant is suggesting that all people are equally intelligent, or have an equal capacity to make moral judgments based on the complicated system his ethics requires, he is saying something very odd. Consider the case of children: do they reason morally as well as adults? The theories of psychologists Jean Piaget and Lawrence Kohlberg suggest they do not. This is hardly a radical notion, but one has to explain why this is so. Their work suggests that abstract moral reasoning is a developed capacity. Like the ability to solve mathematical problems, there are various stages that must be negotiated in moral development. One must be able to add to be able to multiply. Very young children are developmentally incapable of the first, so they are developmentally incapable of the latter. But as children's brains mature they can learn to add, and then to subtract. Through a process of maturation and learning, children can become moral adults. Kohlberg describes six stages of moral development that he divides into three categories of two stages: I. Pre-conventional. II. Conventional. III. Post-conventional. In the first stage morality is conformance to social standards offered by authority figures. In the second stage morality is acting in one's own interest. In the third stage morality is acting to gain social approval. In the fourth stage morality is acting in conformance with law and social custom. The fifth stage is roughly utilitarian, and the sixth stage is roughly Kantian. As the term would suggest, most individuals never evolve past the Conventional stages, few make it to stage five, and almost none make it to stage six. But as this theory reaches its mature view in Kohlberg's work, few children actually grow up to be adult Kantians; many will never get close.[38]

Kantians could, of course, recognize degrees of capacity for moral agency. They further could suggest that even those sentient creatures that have the limited capacity to act on hypothetical or categorical imperatives are still worthy of moral respect. However, this is difficult to square with the historical Kant. But the more important problem is that there seems to be no logical necessity for Kant to have done so. Kant's notion of rationality is broad enough to allow the exclusion of large numbers of sentient creatures from moral consideration. History abounds with examples of ethnocentrists who equate 'different' with 'inferior,' and any moral theory that allows one to label the inferior as beyond moral consideration should be approached skeptically. Thus, Kant's racism, for example, is more than a historical anachronism, and Kantians ignore it at their own peril.

x. BENTHAM AND ANIMALS

Recall that Kant offers us a strict moral dichotomy in the case of animal rights; animals are not ends-in-themselves, and our duties to animals consist solely in not inhibiting human character development. Consider the more nuanced view from Bentham:

> The day has been, I grieve to say in many places it is not yet past, in which the greater part of the species, under the denomination of slaves, have been treated by the law exactly upon the same footing as, in England for example, the inferior races of animals are still. The day *may come*, when the rest of animal creation may acquire those rights which never could have been withholden from them but by the hand of tyranny. The French have already discovered that the blackness of the skin is no reason why a human being should be abandoned without redress to the caprice of a tormentor. It may come one day to be recognized, that the number of the legs, the villosity of the skin, or the termination of the *os sacrum*, are reasons for abandoning a sensitive being to the same fate. What else is it that should trace this insuperable line? Is it the faculty of reason, or, perhaps, the faculty of discourse? But a full-grown horse or dog is beyond comparison a more rational, as well as more conversable animal, than an infant of a day, or a week, or even a month, old. But suppose the case were otherwise, what would it avail? the question is not, Can they *reason*? nor, Can they *talk*? but, Can they *suffer*?[39]

It should be noted that Kant and Bentham are expressing these views at virtually the same time, so it is not that Bentham has any particular historical advantage. Bentham has a completely differing conception of what would cause us to give animals, or people of color for that matter, moral consideration. The importance of this passage is at least twofold. The first is that it is historically one of the earliest justifications and defenses of animal rights. It is probably quoted as often as anything else Bentham has written, and is cited by many contemporary animal rights activists with approval.

Second, Bentham is also making an important theoretical point. Utilitarians must take the suffering of all sentient creatures seriously, and this must offer at least some protection to the disenfranchised. One might argue, however, that this moral consideration is insignificant; when the interests of majorities are considered the suffering of minorities is invariably swamped.

xi. BENTHAM ON PAEDERASTY

But Bentham does not seem to hold this view. Another 'crime' punishable by death during Bentham's era was 'paederasty.' (The modern use of this term often has connotations of child molestation, but Bentham is using it to indicate activities between adults.)

Given the prevailing religious views, it would have been radical to merely suggest a lesser penalty. The American Civil Liberties Union's (ACLU) website indicates that every state in our country had laws against sodomy as recently as 1960. The vast majority did in 1970. Eighteen states still did as recently as 1998. Fourteen states and the Commonwealth of Puerto Rico still did as recently as 2001. These laws were held constitutional by the United States Supreme Court as recently as 1986 in *Bowers* vs. *Hardwick;* the ACLU called this 'perhaps its most notorious decision this century.'[40] Bentham, in a 1785 essay entitled 'Offenses Against One's Self,' argued for the complete decriminalization of all consensual sexual practices among adults, using laws against homosexual sodomy as his chief vehicle. This article was apparently considered so radical (disgusting?) that it was not published until 1978, over one hundred years later, when, of course, it resonated with the modern gay rights agenda. Bentham writes:

> To what class of offences shall we refer these irregularities of the venereal appetite which are stiled unnatural? When hidden from the public eye there could be no colour for placing them any where else: could they find a place any where it would be here. I have been tormenting myself for years to find if possible a sufficient ground for treating them with the severity with which they are treated at this time of day by all European nations: but upon the principle utility I can find none . . . As to any primary mischief, it is evident that it produces no pain in anyone. On the contrary it produces pleasure, and that a pleasure which, by their

> perverted taste, is by this supposition preferred to that pleasure which is in general reputed the greatest. The partners are both willing. If either of them be unwilling, the act is not that which we have here in view: it is an offence totally different in its nature of effects: it is a personal injury; it is a kind of rape . . . As to any secondary mischief, it produces not any pain of apprehension. For what is there in it for any body to be afraid of? By the supposition, those only are the objects of it who choose to be so, who find a pleasure, for so it seems they do, in being so.[41]

Once again, two points suggest themselves. First, Bentham describes his own personal disgust as to what he clearly considers offensive behavior, a view apparently held by the vast majority of Europeans of his era. But Bentham rejects his own and others' intuitions in favor of a strict reliance on the principle of utility. This is not so surprising. But the second point he is making is quite surprising; he seems to suggest that this disgust is not morally important, and whatever painful sensations may be caused by this disgust should be discounted or ignored. He instead relies on the principle of utility in a more reasoned fashion: That is, if these activities do not really cause a balance of pain over pleasure in their practitioners, his own personal disgust is unreasonable. But one of the stock arguments against utilitarianism is that even the irrational feelings of large majorities will trump the behavior of minorities in all cases. If the pain produced by the behavior in the majority outweighs the minority's pleasure, the minority must yield. (A version of this argument, offered by Ronald Dworkin, will be discussed shortly.) Thus, utilitarianism requires that minorities would have to accept the mere prejudices of majorities. Bentham clearly rejects this line of thought. Why is this so? In a less than crystal clear passage he offers a hint:

> Meanwhile the antipathy, whatever it may arise from, produces in persons how many so ever they be in whom it manifests itself, a particular kind of pain as often as the object by which the antipathy is excited presents itself to their thoughts. This pain, whenever it appears, is unquestionably to be placed to the account of the mischief of the offence, and this is one reason for the punishing of it. More than this – upon the view of any pain which these obnoxious persons are made to suffer, a pleasure

> results to those by whom the antipathy is entertained, and this pleasure affords an additional reason for the punishing of it. There remain however two reasons against punishing it. The antipathy in question (and the appetite of malevolence that results from it) as far as it is not warranted by the essential mischieviousness of the offence is grounded only in prejudice. It may therefore be assuaged and reduced to such a measure as to be no longer painful only in bringing to view the considerations which shew it to be ill-grounded. The case is that of the accidental existence of an antipathy which [would have] no foundation [if] the principle of utility were to be admitted as a sufficient reason for gratifying it by the punishment of the object; in a word, if the propensity to punish were admitted in this or any case as a sufficient ground for punishing, one should never know where to stop. Upon monarchical principles, the Sovereign would be in the right to punish any man he did not like; upon popular principles, every man, or at least the majority of each community, would be in the right to punish every man upon no better reason . . . If this were admitted we should be forced to admit the propriety of applying punishment, and that to any amount, to any offence for instance which the government should find a pleasure in comprising under the name of heresy. I see not, I must confess, how a Protestant, or any person who should be for looking upon this ground as a sufficient ground for burning paederasts, could with consistency condemn the Spaniards for burning Moors or the Portuguese for burning Jews: for no paederast can be more odious to a person of unpolluted taste than a Moor is to a Spaniard or a Jew to an orthodox Portuguese.[42]

This passage is hard to swallow. First, Bentham indicates that the pain the majority feels is considerable, caused by the minority behavior, and hardly illusionary. However, if this were justification for punishment, Bentham claims, utilitarianism could not be used to prevent any punishment for any offense. We could hang those individuals who lack good fashion sense, or otherwise offend popular taste. Bentham clearly wishes us to consider this a *reductio ad absurdum* argument against prosecuting paederasts. But many would argue that the obvious conclusion should be to reject utilitarianism. On this line of reasoning, Bentham's own analysis of consensual sodomy demonstrates unequivocably that his utilitarianism is incapable of defending minority rights of any sort. Perhaps this is the killing blow to utilitarianism. Even a cursory reading of Bentham's essay clearly indicates he did not believe this to be a reasonable reading, but perhaps he is simply confused (I will return to this point later). James Q. Wilson actually finds this economical path for rejecting all forms of utilitarianism convincing. In an over three hundred page discussion advocating a rather conservative version of Aristotelian virtue theory, utilitarianism is dismissed 'because Mill's utilitarianism, strictly applied, would justify punishing an innocent man.'[43]

xii. CLASSICAL UTILITARIANISM AND RIGHTS

Wilson's eleven words are hardly an argument, and punishing the innocent is but one example. Of course, the suggestion that a set of theories as diverse as utilitarianism could be shown incapable of supporting any form of rights through one simple example should be doomed to failure. As Alan Gewirth has argued, a single article could not be expected to accomplish such a task. He writes:

> It is well known that there are many varieties of utilitarianism, and this multiplicity is further complicated when we try to place historical utilitarian thinkers under one or another of these varieties. In addition, there are different senses in which utilitarianism, in any of its varieties, may be held to 'justify' certain actions or policies. Also, there are many different kinds of rights, including moral rights, and there are familiar problems about the nature of rights and how their 'existence' can be proved or justified. And, besides all these difficulties, there is the problem of just how rights differ from utilitarian norms. For if the difference between them cannot be clearly established, then it is also difficult to [establish] that 'utilitarianism' is one kind of thing and 'moral rights' another.[44]

But Gewirth's line of reasoning did not deter Rachels, Berry, or Wilson from this truncated line of attack. Wilson's dismissal is truly enlightening. Since he is best known as one of the major conservative voices on crime issues, his example is amazing. Is it now the conservative view of punishment that a criminal justice system that justified punishing an innocent person under any circumstances would be illegitimate? A knee-jerk liberal ACLU member would not make that claim. This issue is usually framed by questions about due process. A better question should be whether a criminal justice system gives due consideration as to whether a defendant's rights have been violated. In a country with a jail and prison population of about two million, it would hardly be credible to suggest that it is possible that all of our prisoners are guilty of the crimes that they have been convicted. One is not required to do extensive research to find cases where innocent individuals have spent decades in prison.[45] Conservatives usually argue that the *continued* incarceration of the innocent is an unfortunate but inevitable price of a functional criminal justice system, and the effort necessary to weed out false claims of innocence from real ones is simply not cost effective.[46] In a similar vein, it would hardly be a credible argument to dismiss the American criminal justice system 'because . . . strictly applied [it] would punish an innocent man.'[47]

Thus, a fair investigation of utilitarianism would ask whether it balances the rights of defendants with other considerations adequately. Bentham clearly believed that utilitarianism could not support punishing adult consensual sexual activity regardless of how many people were offended or how much they were offended. The reason for this clears up what I take to be the gross confusion one finds in Wilson.

Most philosophical movements arise in opposition to some other philosophical movement. For example, logical positivism was an extreme response to some of the grandiose metaphysical speculations of early twentieth century continental thought. The classical utilitarians took their opponents to be what they considered moral intuitionists.[48] The classical utilitarians believed that moral intuitions were often a product of the status quo, and this was a chief hindrance to moral progress. John Stuart Mill thought Bentham's most important insight was to question even our clearest moral intuitions carefully. In an essay critical for understanding Bentham's thought Mill wrote:

> If we were asked to say, in the fewest possible words, what we conceive to be Bentham's place among these great intellectual benefactors of humanity; what he was, and what he was not; what kind of service he did and did not render to truth; we should say he was not a great philosopher, but he was a great reformer in

> philosophy . . . Bentham's method may be shortly described as the method of detail; of treating wholes by separating them into their parts, abstractions by resolving them into Things, classes and generalities by distinguishing them into the individuals of which they are made up; and breaking every question into pieces before attempting to solve it . . . Whatever originality there was in the method – in the subjects he applied it to, and in the rigidity with which he adhered to it, there was the greatest. Hence his interminable classifications. Hence his elaborate demonstrations of the most acknowledged truths. That murder, incendiarism, robbery, are mischievous actions, he will not take for granted without proof; let the thing appear ever so self-evident, he will know the why and the how of it with the last degree of precision . . .[49]

If Mill is correct, and the structure of Bentham's 'Offenses Against One's Self' supports this reading, when Bentham notes that the average Victorian is disgusted by paederasty this is merely a starting point. Bentham wishes to question many of our preconceived intuitions. What makes an activity disgusting? Why is it disgusting? How does this disgust serve anyone's interests? Does this disgust promote utility? Bentham is not suggesting that our moral intuitions are never relevant, but they must be examined closely. Otherwise, we are merely substituting dogma for careful moral reasoning. Mill's analysis of Bentham suggests that Bentham regards unsubstantiated opinions as morally irrelevant. Mill writes:

> He required something more than opinion as a reason for opinion. Whenever he found a phrase used as an argument for or against anything, he insisted upon knowing what it meant; whether it appealed to any standard, or gave intimation of any matter of fact relevant to the question; and if he could not find that it did either, he treated it as an attempt on the part of the disputant to impose his own individual sentiment on other people, without giving them a reason for it; a contrivance for avoiding the obligation of appealing to any external standard, and for prevailing upon the reader to accept of the author's sentiment and opinion as a reason, and that a sufficient one, for itself.[50]

In short, Bentham's view is that unless the moralist's intuitions can be justified, they should be considered of little moral significance. Thus, a sophisticated reading of Bentham offers little support for the claim that the mere feelings of majorities can trump fundamental interests of minorities. Majorities will rule when the principle of utility supports their claims, but this leaves room for minority rights.

xiii. UTILITARIANISM, EGALITARIANISM, AND THE RIGHT TO EQUAL CONSIDERATION

In fact, it should be clear that utilitarianism in all of its forms supports some sort of rights. Historically utilitarianism was a radical theory primarily because of its egalitarianism, not its consequentialism. The idea that the utility of illiterate and landless peasants should be considered on a par with that of the landed aristocracy was shocking in an era barely removed from feudalism. When Bentham advocated moral consideration for animals, and the decriminalization of consensual sex acts, it is not the consequentialist nature of his arguments that was shocking, but that animals or despised minorities should be argued for at all. When Mill argued in behalf of working class women or black slaves, what offended his contemporaries is that white male aristocrats should be morally compelled to modify their behavior in response to claims originating outside their class. And when Peter Singer argues today for massive increases in aid to the third world, vegetarianism, and the ending of factory farms, it is not the consequentialism that enrages his opponents.[51] All these thinkers ask us to expand our definition of the moral community, to find moral consideration where we did not find it before. We are being asked to consider the suffering of those we previously did not consider victims. Clearly, this egalitarianism is a central and essential component to utilitarian thought. Ronald Dworkin has actually argued that this egalitarianism is far more central, far more critical, to whatever intuitive appeal utilitarianism has as a moral theory. Dworkin writes:

> Utilitarianism owes whatever appeal it has to what we might call its egalitarian cast . . . Suppose some version of utilitarianism provided that the preferences of some people were to count for less than those of others in the calculation how best to fulfill

> most preferences overall either because these people were in themselves less worthy or less attractive or less well loved people, or because the preferences in question combined to form a contemptible way of life. This would strike us as flatly unacceptable, and in any case much less appealing than standard forms of utilitarianism. In any of its standard versions, utilitarianism can claim to provide a conception of how government treats people as equals, or, in any case, how government respects the fundamental requirement that it must treat people as equals. Utilitarianism claims that people are treated as equals when the preferences of each, weighted only for intensity, are balanced on the same scales, with no distinctions for persons or merit . . . [a corrupt version of utilitarianism] which gives less weight to some persons than to others, or discounts some preferences because they are ignoble, forfeits that claim. But if utilitarianism in practice is not checked by something like the right to moral independence (and by other allied rights) it will disintegrate, for all practical purposes, into exactly that version.[52]

Dworkin makes explicit and clear an aspect of utilitarianism that is often glossed over. Every commentator notes that utilitarianism has both a consequentialist and a utility promoting component. However, one would hope that any competent commentator should note, at least in passing, that all utilitarians believe, in Bentham's famous utilitarian slogan: Everyone counts as one and only one. As Mill wrote in *Utilitarianism*:

> I must again repeat, what the assailants of utilitarianism seldom have the justice to acknowledge, that the happiness which forms the utilitarian standard of what is right in conduct, is not the agent's own happiness, but that of all concerned. As between his own happiness and that of others, utilitarianism requires him to be as strictly impartial as a disinterested and benevolent spectator. In the golden rule of Jesus of Nazareth, we read the complete spirit of the ethics of utility. To do as you would be done by, and to love your neighbour as yourself, constitute the ideal perfection of utilitarian morality.[53]

Dworkin rightly suggests that this belief is a third essential component of the theory. Thus, utilitarianism is actually a tripartite theory:

stating this explicitly – in a fairly generic form that should include utilitarianism in all its varieties – its three components are:

1. Consequentialist component: practices are evaluated primarily by their consequences. ('Practices' functions here as a generic place holder; Various individual theorists may use acts, actions, rules, processes, procedures, or social systems as a whole, etc. To the best of my knowledge, John Rawls introduced this term.)[54]
2. Utility component: consequences are evaluated by their ability to promote (perhaps maximize) utility. (Utility has also been variously interpreted with pleasure, happiness, or preference satisfaction being most common.)
3. Equal consideration component: every individual's utility is given equal weight; when calculating utility every person's (or sentient creature's) utility is considered as valuable as any other's.

The question then arises: How much weight should one give to this third component? Dworkin's suggestion is we should give it a great deal. In his above passage Dworkin suggests a weak reading of the third component offers a debilitated moral theory. Instead he suggests that utilitarians should adopt what he calls 'the right to moral independence.' As Dworkin describes this:

> People have the right not to suffer disadvantage in the distribution of social goods and opportunities, including disadvantage in the liberties permitted to them by the criminal law, just on the ground that their officials or fellow-citizens think that their opinions about the right way for them to lead their own lives are ignoble or wrong.[55]

If utilitarians are willing to adopt the right to moral independence as a reasonable reading of the right to equal consideration, Dworkin argues that the mere prejudices of majorities are not sufficient to counter other important utilitarian considerations. Dworkin suggests, as a charitable reading of Bentham might, that blind prejudices should be rejected, on utilitarian grounds, as not being worthy of significant moral consideration. If the equal consideration component of utilitarianism is to be taken seriously, it cannot be overridden whenever majorities feel like doing so; there must be some compelling majority interest. In any case, majorities cannot simply be allowed to deny any moral consideration to a despised minority. Dworkin argues that utilitarians cannot simply stand silent when majority persecutors wish to remove their victims from utilitarian calculation. Nazis may wish to deny that Jews are human or worthy of moral consideration, but the utilitarian must deny this. He writes:

> [U]tilitarian theory must be neutral between personal preferences like the preferences for pinball and poetry, as a matter of the theory of justice, it cannot, without contradiction, be neutral between itself and Nazism. It cannot accept at once a duty to defeat the false theory that some people's preferences should count for more than other people's and a duty to strive to fulfill the political preferences of those who passionately accept that false theory, as energetically as it strives for any other preferences. The distinction on which the reply to any argument rests, the distinction between the truth and the fact of the Nazi's political preferences, collapses, because if utilitarianism counts the fact of these preferences, it has denied what it cannot deny, which is that justice requires it to oppose them.[56]

Although his argument is hard to follow in places, Dworkin's major point, as far as it goes, is clear. A utilitarian physicist cannot believe that witches are more real than atoms, simply because the majority loves 'Touched by an Angel.' A utilitarian geologist cannot believe the earth is 5000 years old, simply because a fundamentalist majority would like their religious text to be literally true. Similarly, Dworkin will argue that the utilitarian liberal cannot believe that majorities receive important benefits from their irrational prejudices.

William Galston makes this point very clearly and persuasively. The liberal must recognat all preferences should not be given equal consideration. After all, some individuals have preferences that include the random killing or maiming of others. But there should be room for the acceptance of various conceptions of the good. Galston writes:

> The distinction between good and evil is objective, but the good things of life are heterogeneous, are not neatly rank-ordered, and

> cannot be combined into a single harmonious package. To live well is to choose a good life, which inevitably means excluding other worthy possibilities. The philosophical justification for social pluralism is the diversity of legitimate human goods. This same diversity under girds what I am not alone in regarding as the liberal stance toward life – namely, a generous receptivity to ways of life other than one's own, and a deep commitment to making the effort to understand why others come to embrace outlooks that one regards as peculiar, even repellant.[57]

Thus, a sophisticated liberal must have some criteria for distinguishing other legitimate ways of life from the illegitimate. One approach that could be used by liberal utilitarians is offered by Ronald Dworkin.

Dworkin envisions a society where many members are Sarah-lovers, that is, a group of individuals that value having their own preferences met, but also wish to see Sarah's preferences met.[58] Dworkin suggests that this second preference – the preference for Sarah's preferences – is an illegitimate form of double counting. The Sarah-lover wants his or her preferences counted twice; one for me, one for Sarah. Utilitarianism requires, however, that everyone's preferences must be counted equally. Similarly, Dworkin would find no reason to double count the preferences of a group of paederast-haters. The only exception Dworkin finds for this would be when preferences about other people's preferences are simply essential to meeting your own legitimate needs for safety or security, for example, a society opposed to impaired drivers like 'Mothers Against Drunk Driving.' To return to Bentham's case, on Dworkin's reading the majority has no compelling reasons for hanging paederasts, and obviously enough, everyone has a compelling interest in not being hanged. The only way to justify laws against consensual sex between adults is to apply the utilitarian calculus absurdly; one would have to first find factual evidence that the sexual minority actually harms the majority in some significant sense, overweight the interests of the majority, and then underweight the interests of the minority. Those who are not inclined to take Bentham seriously should examine how well his 'Offenses Against One's Self' shows this to be true.

The obvious problem with Dworkin's example is that it really does not show much. Dworkin has rather grossly stacked the deck.

Since few members of his audience feel anything but revulsion for Nazism, or believe that Nazis gain any legitimate benefits from tormenting their victims (whether they be gypsies, homosexuals, Jews, people of color, communists, liberals, etc.), our moral intuitions (in evaluating this Nazi dominated society) favor the minorities. We cannot seriously entertain the idea that Nazism, in any form, could promote utility. The Nazi also wishes to deny the actual humanity of his or her victims, and to strip them of any moral consideration. Clearly, no moral system could allow that. But not every advocate of majority rule is a Nazi. Similarly, advocates of majority rule do not necessarily deny any moral worth to minorities. Once again, the Nazi is something of a straw person.

All advocates of majority rule should not be painted with this crude brush. There must be some cases where the majorities have compelling interests, and rationally wish to act on those interests after giving minorities due consideration. Do we believe that majorities always win in such cases? If so, in Dworkin's famous phrase, we are not 'taking rights seriously.' If utilitarianism supports majority rule, does it offer tangible benefits to minorities? Can the right to equal consideration offer minorities important protections under a utilitarian system? The Rawlsian animal rights activist Mark Rowlands has suggested that the answer to these questions is no. He writes:

> Utilitarians can embrace the principle of equal consideration only in so far as it maximizes utility, and if the principle of equal consideration should ever clash with the requirement that utility be maximized, it is the former which the utilitarian must sacrifice. Utilitarianism, therefore, does not necessarily treat people with equal consideration; it does so only if such treatment maximizes utility. And this, at least *prima facie*, is not to genuinely accord that person equal consideration at all.[59]

The obvious rejoinder is that as long as minorities have been treated fairly, and their interests taken seriously, we should accept majority rule as democratic and just. But Rowlands finds this answer uncompelling. He writes:

> The utilitarian is likely to reply that considering the interests of all individuals concerned is precisely what it means to treat

> those individuals with equal consideration. And this remains true even when consideration of all affected interests entails, on utilitarian grounds, the sacrifice of certain individuals. Nevertheless, there is a clear divergence between the utilitarian conception of what it means to treat an individual with equal consideration and our intuitive understanding of this notion, and this raises the question of whether utilitarianism is genuinely capable of accounting for the conception of justice embodied in liberal ideology.[60]

Thus, the stage is set. Rowlands tells us that the duty to maximize utility will always trump the right to equal consideration. Dworkin believes that utilitarianism is a rich enough theory to support the right to moral independence. Rowlands argues that the right to equal consideration would be so badly mangled and truncated in utilitarian hands as to be unrecognizable, and clearly no self-respecting liberal political philosopher would support any claim to the opposite. But if Dworkin has no right to claim himself a liberal political philosopher, then probably no one does.

It should be clear that there is a serious tension in any liberal utilitarianism. But as noted by Gewirth earlier, one cannot fruitfully engage this issue at the level of abstraction entertained by Rowlands and Dworkin. It is daunting enough to examine this tension with one thinker and one conception of justice. My purpose in the rest of this dissertation will be to examine this issue in the work of John Stuart Mill. Mill's utilitarianism will be filtered through the work of Rem B. Edwards. In Edwards' view, Mill is a minimizing utilitarian. Thus, part of the answer to Rowlands, and thus to other Rawlsians, is that Mill does not believe that we have an absolute duty to maximize utility. This reduces the tension but does not eliminate it. As Gewirth has noted:

> It is the derivative position of rights in relation to the aggregated sum of utilities that differentiates utilitarianism from principles . . . that directly base rights on the actions-needs of individuals. And it is because of this difference that utilitarianism can provide only accidental justifications for moral rights.[61]

Gewirth wishes to support absolute moral rights. Thus, part of the answer to him is 'so what.' The rights that Gewirth claims utilitarianism cannot support are not supported by even many deontologists, for example, John Rawls. We will see shortly why this is the case. One could also ask why 'accidental justifications' are so obviously illegitimate. Is this a distinction without a difference? If not, it requires some extensive elaboration. Are the 'accidental' justifications one finds in Bentham clearly inferior to the *intuitive* ones found in Kant? No one doubts Kant was a better philosopher than Bentham. If Bentham gets better answers, he must be working with better tools.

One might argue that Mill's utilitarianism is rich enough to support the system of rights he advocated in *On Liberty*, and this system of rights is worth defending. I take this to be a key question in Millian exegesis: Is Mill's moral theory compatible with the system of rights he advocated in On Liberty? However, this question begs the simpler one: Is the system of rights advocated in *On Liberty* worth defending? It is to this question I now turn my attention.

xiv. MODERN ETHICS, UTILITARIANISM, AND KANTIANISM

The modern era also gave us new ways to think about politics and ethics. As noted earlier, the medieval conception of morality and politics rested largely on the authority of religion and the Church. Similar to the rejection of authority in the case of metaphysics and epistemology, the modern philosophers also needed new approaches to value theory.

James Rachels, in his *The Elements of Moral Philosophy*, mentions four which he believes were dominant during the modern era. Rachels writes:

> Ethical Egoism: Each person ought to do whatever will best promote his or her own interests.
>
> Utilitarianism: We ought to do whatever will promote the greatest good for the greatest number.
>
> Kant's theory: Our duty is to follow rules that we could consistently will to be universal laws – that is, rules that we would be willing to have followed by all people in all circumstances.
>
> Social Contract Theory: The right thing to do is to follow the rules that rational, self-interested people can agree to for their mutual benefit.[62]

What all these theories share in common is that they are normative theories of right action. They differ from character- or virtue-based ethic found in ancient Greece. That is, all these theories tell us that we are morally required to perform certain acts. In this sense, all these theories are prescriptive in that they prescribe certain conduct as morally required. So, let us consider whether one should lie to someone else when it will benefit the liar. The ethical egoist will say 'yes,' in fact that is what I am morally required to do. The social contract theorist will likely say 'no,' since it is unlikely that rational, self-interested people would agree to tell lies to each other.

The two theories that dominate most moral debate today are Kantianism and utilitarianism. One reason these theories are dominant is that they square off on a central dilemma that one faces in many ethical decisions. Should we evaluate our conduct by the ends that are produced or by the means that we employ to produce them. Utilitarianism is the theory that dominates the thinking of philosophers today who suggest that we should focus on the ends; similarly, Kantianism tends to dominate among those who suggest we should focus on the means. Thus, utilitarianism is a consequentialist moral theory; actions should be primarily by their consequences. In contrast, Kantianism is a non-consequentialist moral theory that suggests that we look primarily at the means employed.

A second reason that utilitarianism and Kantianism take the main stage. Consider the following case by Bernard Williams:

> Jim finds himself in the central square of a small South American town. Tied up against the wall are a row of twenty Indians, most terrified, a few defiant, in front of them several armed men in uniform. A heavy man in a sweat-stained khaki shirt turns out to be the captain in charge and, after a good deal of questioning of Jim which establishes that he got there by accident while on a botanical expedition, explains that the Indians are a random group of the inhabitants who, after recent acts of protest against the government, are just about to be killed to remind other possible protestors of the advantages of not protesting. However, since Jim is an honoured visitor from another land, the captain is happy to offer him a guest's privilege of killing one of the Indians himself. If Jim accepts, then as a special mark of the occasion, the other Indians will be let off. Of course, if Jim refuses, then there is no special occasion, and Pedro here will do

> what he was about to do when Jim arrived, and kill them all. Jim, with some desperate recollection of schoolboy fiction, wonders whether if he got hold of a gun, he could hold the captain, Pedro and the rest of the soldiers to threat, but it is quite clear from the set-up that nothing of that kind is going to work: any attempt at that sort of thing will mean that all the Indians will be killed, and himself. The men against the wall, and the other villagers, understand the situation, and are obviously begging him to accept. What should he do?[63]

The obvious Kantian answer is no, and the obvious utilitarian answer is yes. It is not clear what either ethical egoism or social contract theory have to say here. The ethical egoist has nothing to gain in either case. Maybe the egoist likes shooting people; maybe she/he does not. Maybe the egoist likes saving people; maybe she/he does not. One problem for social contract theory is that Jim does not live in this society; he has no stake in the outcome. But the more fundamental problem is that if we are to follow rules that reasonable people will agree to, some reasonable people are utilitarians and some reasonable people are Kantians. So why should reasonable people be able to agree in this situation? Social contract theorists such as Rawls are well aware of this problem, and have created ingenious answers. My only point is that they are not obvious in the way that the Kantian and utilitarian answers are. But this kind of mental experiment is useful to make the point I want to take up next.

xv. TWO CONCEPTS OF LIBERTY

In the 1950s, Isaiah Berlin published the highly influential essay 'Two Concepts of Liberty.'[64] He makes a distinction between two concepts of freedom. As explained by Ian Carter:

> Negative liberty is the absence of obstacles, barriers or constraints. One has negative liberty to the extent that actions are available to one in this negative sense. Positive liberty is the possibility of acting – or the fact of acting – in such a way as to take control of one's life and realize one's fundamental purposes. While negative liberty is usually attributed to individual agents, positive liberty is sometimes attributed to collectivities,

> or to individuals considered primarily as members of given collectivities.[65]

Often the debate between supporters of positive liberty and negative liberty becomes quite heated. The extremists in this debate have dominated the literature. So, at the time Berlin was writing in the 1950s, the choice was often mischaracterized as simply a debate between libertarianism and communism. Supporters of positive liberty often argued that negative liberty was a sham. Negative rights are bourgeois rights since under capitalism, humans are so alienated from their humanity that there choices do not reflect their true nature. Just as drug addicts are slaves to their disease, alienated humans under capitalism are slaves to desires emanating from false consciousness. Similarly, supporters of negative liberty often argued that any infringement on individual choice and the free market would lead us down Frederick Hayek's *Road to Serfdom*, and that Franklin Delano Roosevelt's New Deal would ultimately lead us to Stalinist re-education camps.

But these are not the 1950s. In more modest political times, negative liberty is the freedom to be left alone most of the time. Due process rights are an example of negative rights; the government in a liberal democracy places you in prison under rare and clearly identified circumstances. But these rights are not absolute. Thus, most modern societies would reject the Lockian conception of government as the night-watchman state.

On the other hand, governments also have clear obligations to do positive things as well; this is why we have fire departments and schools. There are reasons why the public is willing to pay taxes for armed forces, paramedics, police officers, and firefighters. There are reasons why Social Security in the United States is a popular program widely viewed as successful. There are reasons why the public favors state support for drug treatment programs. There are reasons why health care reform is being debated in the United States as I write. But these rights are not absolute as well. You have no entitlement to perfect safety, a perfect life, or perfect medical care. But most people believe that all of our citizens are entitled to some minimal positive rights. A civilized society does not allow, say, mass starvation, if it can be prevented.

xvi. UNIVERSAL DECLARATION OF HUMAN RIGHTS

This distinction between negative liberty and positive liberty has many important consequences for thinking about both politics and morality. In the political side, is it the primary role of government to leave its citizens alone and only interfere with individual conduct that is directly harming others? Or are there important functions that government provides to its citizens to ensure their well being? Consider the following passages from the United Nations 1948 *Universal Declaration of Human Rights*. In Article 17 we are told that:

> (1) Everyone has the right to own property alone as well as in association with others.
> (2) No one shall be arbitrarily deprived of his property.

However, in Article 25 we are told that:

> (1) Everyone has the right to a standard of living adequate for the health and well-being of himself and of his family, including food, clothing, housing and medical care and necessary social services, and the right to security in the event of unemployment, sickness, disability, widowhood, old age or other lack of livelihood in circumstances beyond his control.
> (2) Motherhood and childhood are entitled to special care and assistance. All children, whether born in or out of wedlock, shall enjoy the same social protection.[66]

The unstated problem the United Nations raises here is clear enough. 'Economic rights' can be cashed out in two distinct ways. In Article 17 we have economic rights cashed out as property rights. If you are the owner of property you have the right not to have it taken from you. Arbitrarily depriving you of your property is a violation of your property rights. Taking your property from you is a violation of your negative right to be left alone.

On the other hand, in Article 25 we have economic rights cashed out as welfare rights. Humans have welfare rights and are thus entitled to a reasonable standard of living. If you lack food, shelter, or medical care, then government has a positive obligation to provide these to you. In particular, we have a clear positive obligation to provide mothers and children with special care and attention. In this case rather than a negative right to be left alone like property rights, welfare rights are rights to have certain social goods provided.

There is, of course, a clear tension here: For the most part, Governments raise revenue by taxing their citizens. Thus, to provide welfare rights to one group of citizens is to deprive other citizens of there property rights. To feed the hungry, it is often necessary to take food from the well off.

Economic rights are a clear example, since the tension between property rights and welfare rights is clear. The tension between civil liberties and public safety is a far more complex issue where negative rights and positive rights come into conflict. It is relatively clear that if governments wish to capture terrorists before they strike, they need good intelligence. But since you do not know who the terrorists are before you begin your investigations, this invariably involves violating the privacy rights of innocent citizens. It would be nice if terrorists and other criminals were easily identified, but in the real world it is often not that simple.

So far, I have been discussing cases where positive rights conflict with negative rights in political terms, and this is how it is ordinarily done. To cash this out in moral terms, one can think of positive duties and negative duties. But this is for reasons I cannot make sense of rarely done. So consider the following mental experiment provided by H.J. McCloskey:

> Suppose a utilitarian were visiting an area in which there was racial strife, and that, during his visit, a Negro rapes a white woman, and that race riots occur as a result of the crime, white mobs, with the connivance of the police, bashing and killing Negroes, etc. Suppose too that our utilitarian is in the area of the crime when it is committed such that his testimony would bring about the conviction of a particular Negro. If he knows that a quick arrest will stop the riots and lynchings, surely, as a utilitarian, he must conclude that he has a duty to bear false witness in order to bring about the punishment of an innocent person.[67]

When McCloskey was writing in 1965, I would consider his views naïve. But what is most striking about this example in a post-September 11, 2001 world is that McCloskey is myopically unconcerned with the victims of the mob who are about to be lynched.

Do they have no rights to be considered? Is there no right to physical safety? Is there absolutely no right to life? While it is clear that those accused of crimes deserve protections from overzealous state authorities, it is also clear that citizens also expect their governments to protect them from terrorists and other criminals. Ignoring any positive obligations to defend the victims of the mob, McCloskey seems to find it easy to resolve the tension between positive and negative obligations in the case above. When one recognizes a right to civil liberties, but no right to public safety, then the issue is simple. Utilitarians are committed to violating rights, therefore utilitarians are moral imbeciles. But if one sees a far more complex world where the rights of one citizen can conflict with another, this simple answer is unsatisfying.

xvii. THE TROLLEY PROBLEM

This type of case has been studied extensively in the literature. For example, the trolley problem has been discussed extensively in the literature by fairly well-known philosophers such as Phillipa Foot, Judith Jarvis Thomson, and Peter Unger. The example provided here is from Science Blogs' Jonah Lehrer. Lehrer writes:

> Suppose you are the driver of a trolley. The trolley rounds a bend, and there come into view ahead five track workmen, who have been repairing the track. The track goes through a bit of a valley at that point, and the sides are steep, so you must stop the trolley if you are to avoid running the five men down. You step on the brakes, but alas they don't work. Now you suddenly see a spur of track leading off to the right. You can turn the trolley onto it, and thus save the five men on the straight track ahead. Unfortunately, there is one track workman on that spur of track. He can no more get off the track in time than the five can, so you will kill him if you turn the trolley onto him. Is it morally permissible for you to turn the trolley?

According to Lehrer, about ninety-five percent the population agree that it is morally acceptable to turn the trolley. So, it seems the majority of people accepts a positive duty to preserve life when one is asked merely to flip a switch. He notes that some philosophers have argued that it would be wrong to not do so, since not turning the trolley will end up killing four more people. But he also asks us to consider this scenario as well:

> You are standing on a footbridge over the trolley track. You can see a trolley hurtling down the track; it's out of control. You turn around to see where the trolley is headed, and there are five workmen on the track . . . What to do? Being an expert on trolleys, you know of one certain way to stop an out-of-control trolley: Drop a really heavy weight in its path. But where to find one? It just so happens that standing next to you on the footbridge is a fat man, a really fat man. He is leaning over the railing, watching the trolley; all you have to do is to give him a little shove, and over the railing he will go, onto the track in the path of the trolley. Would it be permissible for you to do this?

As Lehrer puts it: the 'brute facts' are ultimately unchanged. If we want the five men to live, then we must sacrifice the life of the one. He suggests:

> If our ethical decisions were perfectly rational, then we would act identically in both situations, and would be as willing to push the fat man as we are to turn the trolley. (Kant wouldn't have seen any difference.) And yet, almost nobody is willing to actively throw another person onto the train tracks. The decisions lead to the same outcome, and yet one is moral and one is murder.[68]

In both cases killing the one to save the many is the same. If we belief that moral rights are absolute, and that negative rights always trumps positive rights, then changing the factual circumstances should not change our moral analysis; Kant is correct and both killings are wrong. But Utilitarianism is a moral theory developed by empiricists and naturalists; so one would suspect that as the facts are manipulated slightly, you might get a different sort of analysis. A different set of facts might well bend the balance between the negative right not to be killed and the positive right to be protected. My guess in these cases is that some moral duties such as throwing the fat man in front of the trolley are too onerous to be required by a moral minimilist such as Mill. It is clear from Mill's discussion of Comte that he finds some moral obligations are beyond the call of duty, that is, there are morally desirable acts that are not morally required. This is sometimes referred to by philosophers as supererogation. Mill clearly believes in supererogation. It also seems that some violations of negative rights are too damaging to social cohesion to be easily overridden by positive rights, or to put it another way the positive value of social cohesion cancels out the positive value of additional public safety.

xviii. THE TWO MILLS

As we have seen, Mill as the author of *On Liberty* and *Utilitarianism* has a foot in each camp. This is another way of stating what is sometimes called the two Mills problem, namely: How can Mill's commitment to individual freedom and liberalism be reconciled with lifelong commitment to utilitarianism and the common good? Thus, there is a tension here in Mill's thinking that the supporters of absolute moral rights do not have to face. But this tension is all for the good. Mill's liberal utilitarianism is sympathetic to changing empirical circumstances, and in many cases, this seems relevant. Would you push the fat man in front of the train to save a thousand people? 10,000 people? 100,000 people? 1,000, 000 people including your spouse and children? What if in the final scenario you also knew that the fat man was dying of cancer? What if the fat man is a career criminal, dying of cancer, but not deserving of death? Let's say you were a juror on a capital case where someone is accused of killing a dying career criminal – not deserving of the death penalty – in order to save 1,000,000 people including their spouse and children. Assume also that the defendant did kill the career criminal. Would you vote to convict? Would you vote for death? Could you carry out the execution? Kant's answer is clear. Kant writes:

> Even if civil society resolved to dissolve itself with the consent of all its members – as might be supposed in the case of a people inhabiting an island resolving to separate and scatter throughout the whole world – the last murderer lying in prison ought to be executed before the resolution was carried out. This ought to be done in order that everyone may realize the desert of his deeds, and that the blood-guiltiness may not remain on the people, for otherwise they will all be regarded as participants in the murder as a public violation of justice.[69]

Thus, for Kant the answer to the above question is clear. It is always wrong to kill an innocent person, and anyone who does so should be executed. Consequentialist justification can play no part in moral deliberation. And if no one else is available to do so, each of us has the moral duty to carry out such executions. No exeptions!

Mill must answer that all of these questions involve some degree of supererogation. A liberal society cannot demand that its pacifists kill, but it can recognize the usefulness of allowing its citizens to do so in some cases. And if negative rights are not allowed to trump positive rights in all cases, then there will be times when killing the innocent is acceptable. But it is supererogation tempered with a point made often attributed to Edmund Burke. In an inaugural address delivered to the students of the University of St. Andrews in 1867 Mill says:

> Let not any one pacify his conscience by the delusion that he can do no harm if he takes no part, and forms no opinion. Bad men need nothing more to compass their ends, than that good men should look on and do nothing. He is not a good man who, without a protest, allows wrong to be committed in his name, and with the means which he helps to supply, because he will not trouble himself to use his mind on the subject. It depends on the habit of attending to and looking into public transactions, and on the degree of information and solid judgment respecting them that exists in the community, whether the conduct of the nation as a nation, both within itself and towards others, shall be selfish, corrupt, and tyrannical, or rational and enlightened, just and noble.[70]

Bad things happen when bad people do bad things. Bad things also happen when 'good people' do nothing. This is the lesson of Hurricane Katrina. The residents of New Orleans had a positive right to be helped, and the United States Government was asleep at the wheel. This is a moral truth that Barry, Gewirth, McClosky, Kant, and Kantians in general must ignore. Just as the ancient Pythagoreans had to ignore the irrationality of the square root of two, the Kantians cannot accept that in some situations positive rights must trump negative rights. If the square root of two is not a rational number, that is, an integer divided by an integer, then the purity of numbers is lost. Similarly, if in any conceivable scenario positive rights can trump negative rights, then so goes the Categorical Imperative and absolute moral rights.

Justice, then, is an attempt to balance the rights of all parties who have a stake in the outcome. Some stakeholders have negative rights at stake; some stakeholders have positive rights at stake. If this is so, then as Mill says the indefeasibility of justice is an illusion. In third to last paragraph of *Utilitarianism* he writes:

> It appears from what has been said, that justice is a name for certain moral requirements, which, regarded collectively, stand higher in the scale of social utility, and are therefore of more paramount obligation, than any others; though particular cases may occur in which some other social duty is so important, as to overrule any one of the general maxims of justice. Thus, to save a life, it may not only be allowable, but a duty, to steal, or take by force, the necessary food or medicine, or to kidnap, and compel to officiate, the only qualified medical practitioner. In such cases, as we do not call anything justice which is not a virtue, we usually say, not that justice must give way to some other moral principle, but that what is just in ordinary cases is, by reason of that other principle, not just in the particular case. By this useful accommodation of language, the character of indefeasibility attributed to justice is kept up, and we are saved from the necessity of maintaining that there can be laudable injustice.[71]

Thus, the indefeasibility attributed to justice may be a useful illusion but it is an illusion nonetheless. It is permissible to kidnap the doctor under extraordinary circumstances. His negative rights may be violated, if greater positive rights are at stake. Rights may be overridden when greater rights are at stake. But how do we go about doing this? Mill suggests we use the principle of utility to do so. The liberal utilitarian can support rights and still be a utilitarian at heart. Rights are to be defended, when they are not in conflict with other rights. But when they are, something must be done. In a post-September 11 world, we talk of almost nothing else. How much should be spent for warfare, and how much should be spent on welfare? How many guns and how much butter? And how should we pay for it? Is it fair to soak the rich? Is it fair not to? How much safety do we need and what do we do when safety comes at the price of civil liberties and privacy. What moral requirements must we adhere to when dealing with suspected terrorists? What to do when rights conflict? If you do not accept the use of the principle of utility when rights conflict, then suggest something else asks the utilitarian. Otherwise, you have nothing to contribute of any substance to what may be the pressing moral issues of out time.

NOTES

PREFACE

1. For example, see Himmelfarb 1974. A response to Himmelfarb's two Mills can be found in Ronald Dworkin's 'Liberty and Liberalism,' in Dworkin 1978.
2. Gauss 1997, paragraph 2. Gauss' entry 'Liberalism' is online at http://plato.Stanford.edu/entries/liberalism/.
3. Ibid. paragraph 4.
4. Bowie and Simon 1988, pp. 42–3.

CHAPTER 1: MILL AND THE MODERN WORLD

1. Kolak and Thomson 2006, p. 5.
2. Pojman, 1998.
3. Baird and Kaufman 2008, p. 371.
4. Ibid.
5. Ibid. From Descartes 1641, *Meditations on First Philosophy*, translation by John Cottingham.
6. Kolak and Thomson 2006, p. 384.
7. Ibid.
8. Pojman 2000, pp. 5–7.
9. Sowell 2006, p. 153.
10. Robinson 1995, p. 3.
11. Ibid., pp. 3–4.
12. Skorupski 1998, p. 21.
13. Skorupski 2006, p. 93.
14. Kolak and Thomson 2006, p. 387.
15. Pojman 1998, p. 614.
16. Locke 1975. book I, chapter II, section 2.
17. Ibid., section 3.
18. Ibid., section 4.
19. Nolt 1997, p. 461.
20. Locke 1975, book I, chapter II, section 5.

21. Ibid., chapter III, section 24.
22. Pojman 1998, p. 614.
23. Robinson 1986, p. 327.
24. Skorupski 1989, p. 5.
25. Kitcher 1998, p. 57.
26. Ibid., pp. 57–8.
27. Skorupski 1989, pp. 5–6.
28. Hume 1748, p. 679.
29. Ibid.
30. Morehead and Morehead 1972, p. 152.
31. Ibid., p. 165.
32. This argument is similar to one found in Kolak and Thomson 2006, p. 600.
33. Pojman 1998, p. 775. From Kant 1783, *Prolegomena to any Future Metaphysics*, translation by Paul Carus.
34. Ibid., p. 776.
35. Thomson, 1993, pp. 215–16.
36. Ibid., pp. 216–17, 253–4.
37. Pojman 1998, pp. 771–2.
38. Ibid., p. 772. From Kant 1787, 'Preface' to the 2nd edition of the *Critique of Pure Reason*, translation by Louis Pojman.
39. Ibid.
40. Skorupski 1989, pp. 5–6.
41. Mill 1873, chapter VII, paragraph 4.
42. Ibid.
43. Ibid.
44. Schneewind, 1967, pp. 314–15.
45. Mill, 1843, book VI, chapter 3, paragraph 2.
46. Warren 1920, p. 6.
47. Locke, 1975, book I, chapter I, section 8.
48. Ibid., book II, chapter 1, sections 1–4.
49. Ibid., chapter XXXIII, section 5.
50. Schneewind 1967, p. 16.
51. Warren 1967, p. 82.
52. Mill, James 1869, p. 127.
53. Ibid., p. 82.
54. Ibid., p. 83.
55. Ibid., p. 89.

CHAPTER 2: MILL'S EDUCATION AND EARLY INFLUENCES

1. Mazlish 1975, p. 47.
2. Mill 1873, chapter 1, paragraph 2.
3. Ibid., p. 48, Ball 2005, section 1, paragraph 1.
4. Ball 2005, section 1, paragraph 1.
5. Bain 1882, p. 7.
6. Ball 2005, section 1, paragraph 1.

7. Mazlish 1975, pp. 47–8.
8. Ball 2005, section 1, paragraph 1.
9. Ibid., section 2, paragraphs 1–2.
10. Reeves 2007, p. 12.
11. AB, CW, I, p. 21.
12. Mill 1873, chapter 1, paragraph 4.
13. Ibid.
14. Bain 1882, p. 10.
15. Mill 1873, chapter 3, paragraph 3.
16. Mill 1859, dedication.
17. See Mill 1974, volume XI, p. xxviii for publication details.
18. Ibid., p. 39.
19. Ibid., p. 44.
20. Ibid., p. 42.
21. Ibid., p. 44.
22. Ibid., p. 505.
23. Ibid., pp. 505–6.
24. Ibid., pp. 507–8.
25. Ibid., p. 508.
26. Ibid., p. 508.
27. Ibid., p. 508.
28. Ibid., p. 508.
29. Ibid., pp. 509–10.
30. Ibid., p. 505.
31. Reeve 1998, p. 269.
32. Kolak and Thomson 2006, p. 117. Plato's *Republic*, book IV at 419c, translation by Robin Waterfield.
33. Plato 1956, pp. 61–2 at 356b.

CHAPTER 3: LIBERALISM AND *ON LIBERTY*

1. Schefler 1998, p. 16.
2. Ibid. and Samuelson 1980, p. 41.
3. Ibid.
4. Ibid. and Smith 1937, book IV, chapter 2, paragraph 9.
5. Smith, book IV, chapter 2, paragraph 9.
6. First coined by German scholars, 'das Adam Smith Problem,' in the late nineteenth century. See Teichgraeber 1986, p. xiii and his introduction in general.
7. Smith 1937, pp. 734–6.
8. Book I, chapter 10, paragraph 82.
9. Chapter 2, paragraph 2.
10. Smith, book I, chapter 1, paragraph 3.
11. Ibid.
12. Ibid.
13. Mill 1873, chapter VII, paragraph 19.
14. Ibid.

15. Ibid., paragraph 20.
16. Ibid.
17. Ibid.
18. Ibid.
19. Mill 1859, chapter V, paragraph 4.
20. Mill 1859, chapter 1, paragraph 4.
21. Mill 1859, chapter 1, paragraph 4.
22. Ibid., chapter I, paragraph 15.
23. Ibid., paragraph 11.
24. Rappaport 1974, pp. xv–xvi.
25. Ibid., chapter II, paragraph 17.
26. Ibid., paragraphs 41–4.
27. Ibid., chapter III, paragraph 4.
28. Ibid., paragraph 13.
29. Ibid., paragraph 14.
30. Ibid., chapter II, paragraph 10.
31. Ibid., chapter IV, paragraph 2.
32. Ibid., paragraph 3.
33. Mill 1863, chapter V, paragraphs 24–5.

CHAPTER 4: MILL'S MINIMALIST UTILITARIANISM

1. Rachels 2006.
2. For example, see Scheffler, 1988.
3. Edwards 1986, p. 125.
4. Mill 1843, book VI, chapter 12, section 6, paragraph 2.
5. Edwards 1986, p. 129.
6. Edwards and Graber 1988, p. 13
7. Edwards 1985, p. 183.
8. Edwards and Graber 1988, p. 14.
9. Ibid.
10. Edwards does not explicitly endorse the second feature of Brandt's Ideal rule-utilitarianism, but I assume that he would, since otherwise there would be no reason to think that his utilitarianism is less onerous than Brandt's.
11. Sowell 1985, p. 179. As Sowell's endnote indicates 'There is not one reference to Marx in all of Mill's voluminous writings, nor in his voluminous correspondence.' Ibid., p. 264. See, also, Thomson 1968, p. 51.
12. Urmson 1953, pp. 14–15.
13. Ibid., pp. 14–16.
14. Ibid., p. 17.
15. Ibid.
16. Ibid., p. 24.
17. For a list of authors who read Mill as an act-utilitarian or as a rule-utilitarian see Edwards 1986, p. 135.
18. Mill 1861, chapter 2, paragraph 18.

19. Pojman 1994, p. 252.
20. Kymlicka 1991, p. 48.
21. Callahan 1981, pp. 19–25.
22. Kagan 1991, pp. 1–2.
23. I will leave it as an open question whether it is possible for act-utilitarians or rule-utilitarians to be more moderate than Kagan suggests. That is their problem not mine.
24. Mill 1865, paragraph 9.
25. Kagan 1991, p. 1.
26. Mill 1865, paragraph 9.
27. Ibid., paragraph 12.
28. Ibid., paragraph 14.
29. Mill 1873, chapter VII, paragraphs 27–9.
30. Ibid., paragraphs 16–21.
31. Mill 1859, chapter II, paragraph 13.
32. Lyons 1982, p. 50.
33. Edwards 1985, p. 186.
34. Brown 1974, p. 67.
35. Berger 1984, p. 68.
36. Mill 1861, chapter II, paragraph 2.
37. Packe 1954, p. 17.
38. Berger 1984, pp. 68–9.
39. Mill 1843, book VI, chapter 12, section 5.
40. Ibid., section 6, paragraph 1.
41. Ibid.
42. Ibid., section 7, paragraph 4.
43. Brown 1973a, p. 4.
44. Ibid, p. 5.
45. Edwards 1986, pp. 127–9.
46. Mill 1863, chapter V, paragraph 14.
47. Mill 1838, paragraph 9.
48. Mill 1838, paragraph 62.
49. Mill 1838, paragraph 62.
50. Aristotle. *Nicomachean Ethics*, 1094b 13–27.
51. Mill 1838, paragraph 39.
52. Ryan 1988, p. 255.
53. Mill 1843, book VI, chapter XII, section 7, paragraph 5.
54. See Gray 1996a and 1984b.
55. Rachels 1993, p. 179.
56. Mill 1873, chapter II, paragraph 7. See, also, Semmel 1984, chapter One, and Xenephon 1994, book II, chapter 2, paragraphs 21–34.

CHAPTER 5: MILL AND HUMAN RIGHTS

1. Barry 1986, pp. 56–7.
2. Ibid., p. 56.
3. Kant 1960, pp. 111–13.

4. Hume 1741, p. 213.
5. D'Sousa 1986, chapter Two.
6. Mill 1873, pp. 187–90. Quote on p. 189.
7. Packe 1954, p. 423.
8. Loewen 1996, chapter Six.
9. Mill 1873, Chapter VII, footnote to paragraph 31.
10. Mezciems 1992. From her Introduction to Thomas More's *Utopia*.
11. For example, Chambers 1935, pp. 16–19.
12. Loewen 1996, pp. 165–71.
13. Wright 1996, p. 246.
14. Loewen 1996, p. 170.
15. Chowder 2000, p. 82.
16. Ibid., p. 91. Chowder also wrote 'John Brown's Holy War' the documentary that appeared on PBS's *The American Experience* February 28, 2000.
17. For a review of the severity of the activities committed by activists both for and against expanding slavery into the new territories, see Wright 1996, chapter 24.
18. Kant 1960, p. 51.
19. Ibid., p. 77.
20. Ibid., p. 81.
21. Kant 2009, p. 66. First emphasis mine, second Kant's.
22. Ibid., p. 19.
23. Alexander 1999, p. 267.
24. Packe pp. 56–9.
25. Collins 1997, p. 212.
26. Ibid., p. 213.
27. Ibid.
28. Ibid.
29. Singer 1991, p. 157.
30. Sharpe 1988, p. 146.
31. Jensen 1972.
32. For the claim that intelligence and other achievement tests are the products of a hopelessly elitist or racist ideology, see Lemann 1999. For the claim that they are too limited to be of any practical value, see Gardner 1993, 1995, and 1999. For the denial that there are any innate differences in groups at all, see Dowling 2000.
33. Williams 2001.
34. Sowell 1995, p.70. For a thoughtful and rigorous attempt at refutation of *The Bell Curve*, see Fischer et al., 1996. Incidentally, McWhorter, Williams, and Sowell are all black.
35. Hoff later married the philosopher Fred Sommers and is better known as 'Christina Hoff Sommers.' Hoff 1991, p. 364.
36. Singer 1991, p. 347.
37. Hoff 1991, p. 365.
38. For a thorough and interesting discussion of Piaget, Kohlberg, and the cognitive-developmental school of psychology see Flanagan 1991, chapter 6.

39. Bentham 1789, chapter XVII, section 1, part IV. As cited from Regan and Singer 1989, pp. 25–6.
40. The ACLU's website is www.aclu.org. See specifically http://www.aclu.org/issues/gay/sodomy.html for the statistics cited above. Georgia's Supreme Court invalidated this statute in 1998. The United States Supreme Court finally overturned this decision in 2003.
41. Bentham 1785, pp. 389–90.
42. Ibid., pp. 97–8. Brackets in original.
43. Wilson 1993, p. 239.
44. Gewirth 1982, p. 143.
45. See, Hansen 2001.
46. For examples, one could consider conservative calls to limit writs of habeus corpus, DNA testing of convicts, and appeals based on 'actual innocence.'
47. Wilson 1993, p. 239.
48. See, for example, Mill 1861, chapter One and Mill 1873 as cited earlier in chapter 1.
49. Mill 1838, paragraph 9. 'Bentham' was first published in *London and Westminster Review*, August 1838. Bentham died in 1832 and James Mill in 1836.
50. Ibid., paragraph 10. Bentham's 'Offenses' demonstrates Mill's reading in mind-numbing detail. It includes *fifty* sub-sections.
51. See Singer 2000 for a nice overview of his work.
52. Dworkin 1981, pp. 360–1.
53. Mill, 1863, chapter II, paragraph 17.
54. See Rawls 1955.
55. Dworkin 1981, p. 353.
56. Ibid., p. 363.
57. Galston, 2001.
58. Dworkin, ibid., pp. 365–6.
59. Rowlands 1998, p. 53.
60. Ibid., p. 54.
61. Gewirth 1982, p. 160.
62. Rachels 2006, p. 174.
63. Williams and Smart, 1973, pp. 98–9.
64. The revised edition of this paper is Berlin 1969b.
65. Carter, Ian 2003. Available online at http://plato.stanford.edu/archives/spr2003/entries/liberty-positive-negative/.
66. United Nations 1948.
67. McCloskey 1965.
68. Jonah Lehrer, http://scienceblogs.com/cortex/2007/03/morality_and_war.php.
69. Kant 1965 as cited in Rachels 2006, p. 137.
70. Mill 1867, p. 36.
71. Mill 1861, chapter 5, paragraph 37.

FURTHER READING

PRIMARY SOURCES FOR MILL

Many of Mill's and related works are available online for free. I have used the following:

Classical Utilitarianism: www.laits.utexas.edu/poltheory/cuws/.
The History of Economic Thought: www.newschool.edu/nssr/het/index.htm.
John Stuart Mill Links: www.utilitarian.net/jsmill.
Utilitarianism.Org: www.utilitarianism.org/one.html.

There are many others. There is now a standard edition of Mill's work used by Mill scholars. It is first rate. *The Collected Works of John Stuart Mill* can be found in many university libraries, and the bibliographic information for this work and others I will mention are in the accompanying bibliography. See Mill 1974.

There are also many reasonably priced paperback editions that I have found useful. For example, the following are inexpensive and have useful additions by their editors:

Mary Warnock's anthology *Utilitarianism and Other Essays*. This fine collection includes excerpts from Bentham and John Austin, along with Mill's 'Bentham,' *Utilitarianism*, and *On Liberty*, and an essay by the editor (see Mill).

John Gray's *On Liberty and Other Essays*. It includes *On Liberty, Utilitarianism, Considerations on Representative Government*, and *The Subjection of Women* along with a useful essay by the editor. See Mill 2008.

Another work I can recommend is Steven Collini's *On Liberty and Other Writings*. It includes *The Subjection of Women, On Liberty*, and *Chapters on Socialism* along with an essay by the editor. See Mill 1989.

Mill's feminism is represented in Alice Rossi's *Essays on Sex Equality*. It includes along with *The Subjection of Women*, an essay by Mill and Harriet Taylor Mill on marriage and divorce along with an essay 'Enfranchisement of Women' by Harriet Taylor Mill. For those who want to study the 'Harriet problem,' this is one place to start. Rossi has included her own excellent 63 page discussion of Mill's liberal feminism. See Mill and Mill 1970.

Jonathan Riley's *Principals of Political Economy* has excerpts from the title along with *Chapters on Socialism* and an essay by the editor. This is a good introduction to Mill's economic thought. See Mill 1996.

Elizabeth Rappaporte's *On Liberty*, George Sher's *Utilitarianism* and John Robson's *Autobiography* are the versions I use regularly. See Mill 1978, Mill 1979 and Mill 1989b.

SCHOLARLY SECONDARY SOURCES FOR MILL

For serious students of Mill I can recommend the following:

John Skorupski's *John Stuart Mill*. I consider this the best attempt to give a comprehensive look at all aspects of Mill's philosophy. See Skorupski 1989. His edited anthology *The Cambridge Companion* to Mill is also comprehensive. Many important Mill scholars have contributed articles on diverse topics. See Skorupski 1998.

Jonathan Riley's *Liberal Utilitarianism* is a thoughtful look at Bentham, Mill, and what it means to be a liberal utilitarian. See Riley 1988.

I also recommend John Gray's *Mill on Liberty*, Fred Berger's *Happiness, Justice and Freedom*, John Robson's *The Improvement of Mankind*, Alan Ryan's *The Philosophy of John Stuart Mill*, and Wendy Donner's *The Liberal Self*. See Gray 1996 Berger 1984, Robson 1968, Ryan 1988, and Donner 1991.

Two anthologies that contain interesting articles are Shneewind 1969 and Gorovitz 1971. Shneewind includes articles on many aspects of Mill's thought. Gorovitz focuses on ethical theory. It also includes the full text of *Utilitarianism* and Book VI, Chapter 12 of *A System of Logic*.

EASIER READING

John Skorupski's *Why Read Mill Today?* is a very accessible overview of Mill. For an introductory look at *On Liberty* I recommend Jonathan Riley's *Mill on Liberty*.

For another overview focused on Mill's ethics and politics I recommend Susan Anderson's *On Mill*. See Skorupski 2008, Riley 1998, and Anderson 2000.

BIOGRAPHIES

I have read four biographies of Mill and I found each is useful in its own way. Packe 1954 contains a great deal of information, but he is more of a historian than a philosopher. Mazlish 1975 is thought provoking look at the relationship between James and John Stuart Mill, but only if one can handle a Freudian approach. Capaldi 2004 is the best of the bunch, but the close second Reeves 2007 is a livelier read.

BIBLIOGRAPHY

Ackrill, J.L. 1981. *Aristotle the Philosopher*. New York: Oxford University Press.

Alexander, Natelie. 1999. 'Sublime Impersonation: The Rhetoric of Personification in Kant.' In Hendricks and Oliver 1999.

Anderson, Susan L. 2000. *On Mill*. Belmont, CA: Wadsworth.

Baird, Forrest E. and Walter Kaufman. 2008. *From Plato to Derrida*. New York: Pearson Prentice Hall.

Baker, John M. 1971. 'Utilitarianism and "Secondary Principles".' *Philosophical Quarterly* 21, no. 81, 69–71.

Bayles, Michael D., ed. 1968. *Contemporary Utilitarianism*. Anchor Books, Garden City, NJ.

Barry, Vincent. 1986. *Moral Issues in Business*. Belmont, CA: Wadsworth.

Bentham, Jeremy. 1785. 'Offenses Against One's Self.' *Journal of Homosexuality* 3, 389–405.

Bentham, Jeremy. 1795. 'Supply Without Burthen.' In Bentham 1952.

Bentham, Jeremy. 1952. *Jeremy Bentham's Economic Writings*. Vol. 1. Great Britain: Blackfriars Press.

Bentham, Jeremy. 1970. 'Anarchical Follies.' In Melden 1970.

Bentham, Jeremy. 1982. *An Introduction to the Principles of Morals and Legislation*. New York: Methuen Press.

Berger, Fred. 1984. *Happiness, Justice and Freedom: Central Themes in the Moral and Political Philosophy of John Stuart Mill*. Berkeley, CA: University of California Press.

Berlin Isaiah. 1969a. *Four Essays on Liberty*. London: Oxford University Press.

Berlin Isaiah. 1969b. 'Two Concepts of Liberty.' In Berlin 1969a.

Bowie, Norman E. and Robert L. Simon. 1978. *The Individual and the Political Order: An Introduction to Social and Political Philosophy*. 2nd ed. Englewood Cliffs, NJ: Prentice-Hall.

Brown, D.G. 1972. 'Mill on Liberty and Morality.' *The Philosophical Review* 81, 133–58.

Brown, D.G. 1973a. 'What is Mill's Principle of Utility?' *Canadian Journal of Philosophy* 3, 1–12.

Brown, D.G. 1973b. 'John Rawls: John Mill.' *Dialogue* 12, 477–9.

Brown, D.G. 1974. 'Mill's Act-Utilitarianism.' *The Philosophical Quarterly* 24, 67–8.
Callahan, Daniel. 1981. 'Minimal Ethics: On the Pacification of Morality.' *Hastings Center Report*. October.
Capaldi, Nicholas. 2004. *John Stuart Mill*. New York: Cambridge University Press.
Cargile, James. 1971. 'Utilitarianism and the Desert Island Problem.' In Gorovitz 1971.
Carter, Ian. 2003. 'Positive and Negative Liberty.' *The Stanford Encyclopedia of Philosophy*, Spring.
Chowder, Ken. 2000. 'The Father of American Terrorism.' *American Heritage*, February/March.
Clor, Harry M. 1985. 'Mill and Millians on Liberty and Moral Character.' *The Review of Politics* 47, no. 1: 3–26.
Collins, Georg Ludwig. 1997. 'From the Lectures of Professor Kant: Konigsberg, Winter Semester, 1784–5.' In Kant 1997.
Copley, Stephen and Kathryn Sutherland, eds. 1995. *Adam Smith's Wealth of Nations: New Interdisciplinary Essays*. New York: Manchester University Press.
Cozic, Charles P., ed. 1995. *Sexual Values: Opposing Viewpoints*. San Diego, CA: Greenhaven Press.
de Waal, Frans. 1982. *Chimpanzee Politics: Power and Sex among Apes*. New York: Harper and Row.
Donner, Wendy. 1991. *The Liberal Self: John Stuart Mill's Moral and Political Philosophy*. Ithica, NY: Cornell University Press.
Donner, Wendy. 1998. 'Mill's Utilitarianism.' In Skorupski 1998.
Dowling, Collette. 2000. *The Frailty Myth: Women Approaching Physical Equality*. New York: Random House.
D'Sousa, Dinesh. 1995. *The End of Racism: Principles for a Multiracial Society*. New York: The Free Press.
Dworkin, Ronald W. 1978. *Taking Rights Seriously*. Cambridge, MA: Harvard University Press.
Dworkin, Ronald W. 1985. *A Matter of Principle*. Cambridge, MA: Harvard University Press.
Edwards, Paul, ed. 1967. *The Encyclopedia of Philosophy*. New York: Crowell Collier and Macmillan.
Edwards, Rem B. 1985. 'J. S. Mill and Robert Veatch's Critique of Utilitarianism.' *Southern Journal of Philosophy* 23, no. 2, 181–200.
Edwards, Rem B. 1986. 'The Principle of Utility and Mill's Minimizing Utilitarianism.' *Journal of Value Inquiry* 20, 125–36.
Edwards, Rem B. and Glenn C. Graber. 1988. *Bio-ethics*. New York: Harcourt Brace Jovanovich.
Fancher, Raymond E. 1985. *The Intelligence Men: The Makers of the I.Q. Controversy*. New York: W.W. Norton.
Fischer, Claude S., Michael Hout, Martin Sanchez Jankowski, Samuel R. Lucas, Ann Swidler, and Kim Voss. 1996. *Inequality by Design: Cracking the Bell Curve Myth*. Princeton, NJ: Princeton University Press.

Flanagan, Owen. 1991. *The Science of the Mind*. Cambridge, MA: MIT Press.

Fraser, Steven, ed. 1995. *The Bell Curve Wars: Race Intelligence, and the Future of America*. New York: Basic Books.

Gauss, Gerald. 1997. 'Liberalism.' *The Stanford Internet Encyclopedia of Philosophy*. http://plato.Stanford.edu/entries/liberalism/.

Gardner, Howard. 1993. *Frames of Mind: The Theory of Multiple Intelligences*. New York: Basic Books.

Gardner, Howard. 1995. 'Cracking Open the IQ Box.' In Fraser 1995.

Gorovitz, Samuel, ed. 1971. *Utilitarianism with Critical Essays*. Indianapolis, IN: Bobbs-Merrill.

Gray, John. 1996. *Mill on Liberty: A Defense*. 2nd ed. New York: Routledge.

Heilbroner, Robert L. 1962. *The Worldly Philosophers*. New York: Time.

Hendricks, Christina and Kelly Oliver. 1999. *Language and Liberation: Feminism, Philosophy, and Language*. Albany, NY: State University of New York Press.

Herrstein, Richard J. and Charles A. Murray. 1994. *The Bell Curve: Intelligence and Class Structure in American Life*. New York: The Free Press.

Himmellfarb, Gertrude. 1974. *On Liberty and Liberalism: The Case of John Stuart Mill*. New York: Alfred A. Knopf.

Hobbes, Thomas. 1621. *Leviathan*. In Kolak and Thomson 2006.

Hoff, Christina. 1991. 'Immoral and Moral Uses of Animals.' In Olen and Barry 1991.

Hume, David. 1741. *Essays, Moral, Political and Literary*. New York, NY: Alfred A. Knopf.

Hurley, Patrick J. 2003. *A Concise Introduction to Logic*. 8th ed. Belmont, CA: Wadsworth/Thomson Learning.

Jensen, Arhur R. 1972. *Educability and Group Differences*. New York: Harper and Row.

Kagan, Shelly. 1991. *The Limits of Morality*. New York: Oxford University Press.

Kant, Immanuel. 1960. *Observations on the Feeling of the Beautiful and Sublime*. Berkeley, CA: University of California Press.

Kant, Immanuel. 1997. *Lectures on Ethics: The Cambridge Edition of the Works of Immanuel Kant*. Cambridge: Cambridge University Press.

Kant, Immanuel. 2009. *Groundwork of the Metaphysic of Morals*. Translated and analyzed by H. J. Patton. New York: Harper Perennial Modern Thought.

Kolak, Daniel and Garrett Thomson. 2006. *The Longman Standard History of Philosophy*. New York: Pearson Longman.

Kymlicka, Will. 1989. *Liberalism, Community and Culture*. New York: Oxford University Press.

Lemann, Nicholas. 1999. *The Big Test: The Secret History of the American Meritocracy*. New York: Farrar, Straus, and Garoux.

Loewen, James W. 1996. *Lies My Teacher Told Me: Everything Your American History Textbook Got Wrong*. New York: Simon and Schuster.

Lyons, David. 1994. Rights, Welfare, and Mill's Moral Theory. New York: Oxford University Press.

Mazlish, Bruce. 1975. *James and John Stuart Mill: Father and Son in the Nineteenth Century*. New York: Basic Books.
McWhorter, John H. 2000. *Losing the Race: Self-sabotage in Black America*. New York: The Free Press.
Melden, A.I., ed. 1970. *Human Rights*. Belmont, CA: Wadsworth.
Mezciems, Jenny. 1992. 'Introduction.' In More 1992.
Mill, John Stuart. 1838. 'Bentham.' In Mill 1974.
Mill, John Stuart. 1843. *A System of Logic*. In Mill 1974.
Mill, John Stuart. 1848. *Principles of Political Economy*. In Mill 1974.
Mill, John Stuart. 1859. *On Liberty*. In Mill 1974.
Mill, John Stuart. 1861. *Utilitarianism*. In Mill 1974.
Mill, John Stuart. 1865. 'The Later Speculations of Auguste Compte.' In Mill 1974.
Mill, John Stuart. 1867. *Inaugural Address: Delivered to the University of St. Andrews, February 1, 1867*. London: Longmans, Green, Render, and Dyer.
Mill, John Stuart. 1873. *The Autobiography of John Stuart Mill*. In Mill 1974.
Mill, John Stuart. 1974. *Collected Works of John Stuart Mill*. Toronto and Buffalo: University of Toronto Press.
Mill, John Stuart. 1978. *On Liberty*. Indianapolis, IN: Hackett.
Mill, John Stuart. 1979. *Utilitarianism*. Indianapolis, IN: Hackett books.
Mill, John Stuart. 1989a. *Autobiography*. London: Penguin Classics.
Mill, John Stuart. 1989b. *On Liberty and Other Writings*. New York: Cambridge University Press.
Mill, John Stuart. 1991. *On Liberty and Other Essays*. New York: Oxford University Press.
Mill, John Stuart. 1994. *Principles of Political Economy and Chapters on Socialism*. New York: Oxford University Press.
Mill, John Stuart. 2008. *On Liberty and Other Essays*. New York: Oxford University Press.
Mill, John Stuart and Harriet Taylor Mill. 1970. *Essays on Sex Equality*. Chicago, IL: University of Chicago Press.
More, Thomas. 1992. *Utopia*. New York: Alfred A. Knopf.
Nolt, John E. 1997. *Logics*. Belmont, CA: Wadsworth.
Olen, Jeffrey and Vincent Barry, eds. 1991. *Applying Ethics: A Text with Readings*. Belmont, CA: Wadsworth Publishing Co.
Packe, Michael St. John. 1954. *The Life of John Stuart Mill*. New York: Macmillan.
Plato. 1956. *Protagoras*. Translation by Benjamin Jowett, with extensive revision by Martin Ostwald, and edited, with an introduction, by Gregory Vlastos. Indianapolis, IN: The Boobs-Merrill Company.
Plato. 1993. *Republic*. In Kolak and Thomson 2006.
Pojman, Louis P. 1990. *Ethics: Discovering Right and Wrong*. Belmont, CA: Wadsworth.
Pojman, Louis P. 1998. *Classics of Philosophy*. New York: Oxford University Press.

Pojman, Louis P. 2000. *Introduction to Philosophy: Classical and Contemporary Readings*. Belmont, CA: Wadsworth/Thomson Learning.
Rachels, James. 2006. *The Elements of Moral Philosophy*. 5th ed. Edited and revised by Stuart Rachels. Boston, MA: McGraw-Hill.
Rapaport, Elizabeth. 1978. 'Editor's introduction.' In Mill 1978.
Rawls, John. 1955. 'Two Concepts of Rules.' In Gorovitz 1971.
Rawls, John. 1971a. 'Justice as Reciprocity.' In Gorovitz 1971.
Rawls, John. 1971b. *A Theory of Justice*. Cambridge, MA: The Belknap Press of Harvard University Press.
Rawls, John. 1993. *Political Liberalism*. New York: Cambridge University Press.
Regan, Tom and Peter Singer. 1989. *Animal Rights and Human Obligations*. Englewood Cliffs, NJ: Prentice Hall.
Reeve, C.D.C. 1988. *Philosopher-kings: The Argument of Plato's Republic*. Princeton, NJ: Princeton University Press.
Reeves, Richard. 2007. *John Stuart Mill: Victorian Firebrand*. London: Atlantic Books.
Riley, Jonathan. 1988. *Liberal Utilitarianism: Social Choice Theory and J.S. Mill's Philosophy*. New York: Cambridge University Press.
Riley, Jonathan. 1989. 'Rights to Liberty in Purely Private Matters.' *Economics and Philosophy* 5, 121–66.
Riley, Jonathan. 1991. 'One Very Simple Principle.' *Utilitas* 3, 1–35.
Riley, Jonathan. 1994. 'Editor's Introduction.' In Mill 1994.
Riley, Jonathan. 1996. 'J. S. Mill's Utilitarian Assessment of Capitalism Versus Socialism.' *Utilitas* 8, 1.
Riley, Jonathan. 1998a. 'Mill's Political Economy: Ricardian Science and Liberal Utilitarian Art.' In Skorupski 1998.
Riley, Jonathan. 1998b. *Mill on Liberty*. New York: Routledge.
Ring, Jennifer. 1985. 'Mill's the Subjection of Women: The Methodological Limits of Liberal Feminism.' *The Review of Politics* 47, 27–44.
Robinson, Daniel N. 1982. *Toward a Science of Human Nature*. New York: Columbia University Press.
Robinson, Daniel N. 1986. *An Intellectual History of Psychology*. Madison, WI: Wisconsin University Press.
Robinson, Timothy A. 1995. *Aristotle in Outline*. Indianapolis, IN: Hacket.
Robson, John M. 1968. *The Improvement of Mankind: The Social and Political Thought of John Stuart Mill*. Toronto: University of Toronto Press.
Rowlands, Mark. 1998. *Animal Rights: A Philosophical Defence*. New York: St. Martin's Press.
Ryan, Alan, ed. 1979. *The Idea of Freedom: Essays in Honour of Isaiah Berlin*. Oxford University Press.
Ryan, Alan. 1988. *The Philosophy of John Stuart Mill*. New York: Pantheon Books.
Ryan, Alan. 1998. 'Mill in a Liberal Landscape.' In Skorupski 1998.
Samuelson, Paul A. 1980. *Economics*. New York: McGraw-Hill.
Scheffler, Samuel. 1988. *Consequentialism and its Critics*. Great Britain: Oxford University Press.

Schlefer, Jonathan. 1998. 'Today's Most Mischievous Misquotation.' *Atlantic Monthly*, March.
Sharpe, Robert. 1988. *The Cruel Deception*. London: Thorsens.
Singer, Peter. 1972. 'Famine, Affluence, and Morality.' In Sommers 1985.
Singer, Peter. 1979a. *Practical Ethics*. Cambridge, MA: Cambridge University Press.
Singer, Peter. 1979b. 'Without Virtue.' In Sommers 1985.
Singer, Peter. 1986. 'Morality, Egoism, and the Prisoner's Dilemma.' In Sommers 1986.
Singer, Peter. 1989. 'Down on the Factory Farm.' In Regan and Singer 1989.
Singer, Peter. 1991. 'All Animals are Equal.' In Olen and Barry 1991.
Singer, Peter. 1999. 'The Singer Solution to World Hunger.' *New York Times*, September 5.
Singer, Peter. 2000. *Writings on an Ethical Life*. New York: The Ecco Press.
Skinner, Andrew S. 1995. 'Adam Smith and the Role of the State: Education as a Public Service.' In Copley and Sutherland 1995.
Skorupski, John. 1989. *John Stuart Mill*. New York: Routledge.
Skorupski, John, ed. 1998. *Cambridge Companion to Mill*. New York: Cambridge University Press.
Skorupski, John. 2006. *Why Read Mill Today?* New York: Routledge.
Smith, Adam. 1937. *Inquiry into the Nature and Causes of the Wealth of Nations*. New York: The Modern Library.
Smith, Adam. 1966. *The Theory of Moral Sentiments*. New York: Augusta M. Kelley.
Sommers, Christina Hoff, ed. 1985. *Vice and Virtue in Everyday Life: Introductory Readings in Ethics*. New York: Harcourt Brace and Jovanovich.
Sommers, Christina Hoff, ed. 1986. *Right and Wrong: Basic Readings in Ethics*. New York: Harcourt Brace Jovanovich.
Sowell, Thomas. 1972. *Say's Law: An Historical Analysis*. Princeton, NJ: Princeton University Press.
Sowell, Thomas. 1974. *Classical Economics Reconsidered*. Princeton, NJ: Princeton University Press.
Sowell, Thomas. 1985. *Marxism: Philosophy and Economics*. New York: Quill.
Sowell, Thomas. 1995. 'Ethnicity and IQ.' In Fraser 1995.
Sowell, Thomas. 2006. *On Classical Economics*. New Haven, CT: Yale University Press.
Steintrager, James. 1977. *Bentham*. Ithaca, NY: Cornell University Press.
Stewart, Robert M., ed. 1986. *Readings in Social and Political Philosophy*. New York: Oxford University Press.
Strossen, Nadine. 1995. *Defending Pornography: Free Speech, Sex, and the Fight for Women's Rights*. New York: Scribner.
Taylor, Charles. 'What's Wrong with Negative Liberty?' In Ryan 1978.
Teichgraeber, Richard F. 1986. *'Free Trade' and Moral Philosophy: Rethinking the Sources of Adam Smith's Wealth of Nations*. Durham, NC: Duke University Press.
Ten, C.L. 1971. 'Mill on Self-Regarding Actions.' In Gorovitz 1971.

Thomson, Garrett. 1993. *An Introduction to Modern Philosophy*. Belmont, CA: Wadsworth.

Thomson, Garrett. 2001. *On Locke*. Belmont, CA: Wadsworth/Thomson Learning.

Urmson, J.O. 1953. 'The Interpretation of the Moral Philosophy of J. S. Mill.' In Bayles 1968.

Van De Pitte, Frederick Patrick. 1971. *Kant as Philosophical Anthropologist*. The Hague: Martinus Nijhoff.

Weinstock, Daniel M. 1996. 'Making Sense of Mill.' *Dialogue* 35, 791–804.

Williams, Bernard and J. C. C. Smart. 1973. *Utilitarianism: For and Against*. Cambridge University Press.

Wilson, James Q. 1975. *Thinking about Crime*. New York: Basic Books.

Wilson, James Q. 1983. 'Thinking about Crime: The Debate over Deterrence.' *Atlantic Monthly*, September.

Wilson, James Q. 1993. *The Moral Sense*. New York: The Free Press.

Wilson, James Q. and George L. Kelling. 1982. 'Broken Windows: The Police and Neighborhood Safety.' *Atlantic Monthly*, March.

Wilson, James Q. and George L. Kelling. 1989. 'Making Neighborhoods Safe.' *Atlantic Monthly*, February.

Worth, Robert. 1995. 'A Model Prison.' *Atlantic Monthly*, November.

Wright, Mike. 1996. *What They Didn't Teach You about the Civil War*. Novato, CA: Presidio Press.

Xenophon. 1994. *Memorabelia*. Ithaca, NY: Cornell University Press.

Yohe, Gary W. 1985. *Study Guide to Accompany Samuelson and Nordhaus: Economics*. New York: McGraw-Hill.

INDEX